A TRAUMATIC BRAIN INJURY:

A MOM'S VIEW OF A MIRACLE

Linda Tegeler

PRESS

A Traumatic Brain Injury:
A Mom's View of a Miracle
by Linda Tegeler

Printed in the United States of America

ISBN 978-1-60266-955-0

Unless otherwise indicated, Bible quotations are taken from Ryrie Study Bible, New American Standard version. Copyright © 1995 by Moody Press.

www.xulonpress.com

Dedicated to Craig...

Who worked so hard to regain his life,

overcome his fears,

and hang on to his faith in Jesus.

Acknowledgements

This book was inspired by a nurse who encouraged me to keep a journal while our son was in PICU (Pediatric Intensive Care Unit) at a trauma center after Craig sustained a TBI (Traumatic Brain Injury) from an automobile accident on May 21, 1994, during his sophomore year in high school.

I wanted to write it to help other families who had loved ones with a head injury and explain how we waited, watched, hoped, and walked through the days and months ahead. We are born-again Christians, and I wanted the journal to help other Christians stand on God's promises the way we stood on them while we waited upon the Lord!

There are deep, dark valleys we all must walk through, and I wanted Craig to know how God provided for us/him, about His promises to us, and the journey we made! After a few years, my heart's desire sort of changed. Now, my heart's desire is just to record my view from his bedside: how God worked, how He walked us through this tragedy, all the promises He fulfilled, and the miracle He worked in my son's life.

Craig, this is your recorded journey from *mom's* view at your bedside, and later as your cheerleader at life's sidelines. My heart's desire is that you never, never forget what God did and what we learned, as we march on in our journey…called

Life, remembering the past and Who brought us through it as we press on towards the goal!!

Love,
     Mom

CRAIG'S STORY

A Mother's Account of His Journey Back

Craig, you asked me to rewrite your journal and put in "all the details" and promises God gave us along the way. I'll try! I stand in awe of what God did for you and for us during "this storm" in your life and in our lives. God spoke! God displayed Himself and we saw His wonders and miracles. He taught us to wait, to listen, and to expect.

I applaud you for your hard work in rehab: doing triple therapies and then persevering in spite of some things that happened along the way. You have learned there is a spiritual side to life. You have learned God is in control of even the bad things that happen, and He **will** lead his children through the pain, the questions-all of it! We have found that it is in the storm where we learn who Jesus really is!

Love, Forever and Always,
Mom

Dear Craig,

This is Your Journey Back

Saturday, May 21, 1994

It was an ordinary Saturday night; you and your brother Mike had gone to a Fellowship of Christian Athletes Bible study at a nearby friend's house. After the study, you called us to let us know you were taking your girlfriend home in your Dad's new Ford truck. It was a beautiful spring night, and you made it to Whitewater Road about a mile from her house. Dad and I were watching <u>Dr. Quinn, Medicine Woman</u> on television at about 8:30 p.m. We got a call from a farmer who lived on Whitewater Road. He told us to come to Whitewater Road, west of Gifford; there had been an accident. We tried to call your girlfriend's parents twice. Our hearts started praying immediately: "Be there Lord, Let it be simple." I wondered if it would be a broken arm or leg if it would be bad! It's ironic what each of us considers bad. We just asked the Lord to be with everyone involved!

As we approached the scene of the accident, the road was blocked off but rescue trucks let us through to another roadblock, where a Wayne County police officer was situated. Dad told me to wait while he got out and talked to him. I said there was only one question to ask: "Is Craig awake?" The officer lowered his head and looked towards the pavement, avoiding eye contact. He told us to go to the Emergency Room at our local hospital **immediately**! I knew it was worse than we figured, hoped against, or imagined. Dad didn't waste any time getting us there. One of our friends who works in the Emergency Department came out of the trauma room, looking stressed and hurried, to ask about your allergies and medicines. We kept thinking, "This can't be happening; this is a bad dream, and we'll wake up."

We set about giving your information to the staff in Admitting, and then we were ushered into a side waiting room. Another sign things are not good is not being put in the main waiting room. As an LPN, I sat with families while they waited for that news. The trauma doctor joined us in that little room, introduced himself, and said that you had a head injury. You were unconscious, and on your way to X-ray for a CT scan. He requested permission to put a trauma transport helicopter in the air to transfer you as soon as possible, since time was of the essence. We said yes, and he disappeared. My heart raced...wondering who I needed to call, how much money I needed to get, etc. I called a friend to borrow some money. I called Aunt Becky, but she wasn't home. I called Aunt Claudia and told her what had happened. Craig's FCA leader, Heidi, came. In just a few minutes, the Emergency Department staff said we could see you.

Dad and I went in; Heidi came too. You were breathing through an intubation tube attached to an ambu bag, and a person stood at your head ambuing you. Craig, my nursing skills kicked in as I started assessing you physically. Your skin color was good, but you were struggling physically. Your abdomen was really distended from excess air, you were cold and shivering, and your arms looked somewhat rigid secured under a safety strap. Jill, our pastor's wife, appeared from somewhere. We followed you to X-ray for your first CT scan. I knew several people assisting with your care; they all looked stressed and worried! I cried while waiting for your x-ray. I knew you were critical. Dad hugged me, while we waited. Our neighbor's daughter (Betsy) from down the road took your CT. She came out, gave us a hug, and wished us well. When we came back through X-ray, we saw April, your girlfriend, laying on a stretcher a couple of bay areas down from you. She was awake and looked okay physically. She looked so afraid, so we prayed for her. Craig, my burden was for you! We prayed for April on our journey to see you, but it was as if the Lord said she was okay.

We (Pastor Dave, his wife Jill, FCA sponsor Heidi, friend Teresa, your brother Mike, your Dad, and I) formed a prayer circle in the bay area next to your stretcher. We prayed specifi- cally that God would make **all** the decisions. Your best friend Teddy and his mother Virginia were waiting in the lobby. Aunt Claudia appeared, gave me a hug, and came in to see you before we left for Indy. Virginia came in to see you, but I felt it best that Teddy not see you. This upset Teddy, we later found out; but **if** you didn't make it, I wanted Teddy to have all good memories and not that one horrendous memory of the way you looked in the Emergency Department.

We went out briefly, while they finished getting you ready. The waiting room was full of people who knew you, April, and our families. I saw a lot of faces (but a lot of this is a blur). I remember Debbie (a family friend) giving me a hug and Virginia (Theo's mom), but I just remember being led here or there. Your trauma doctor called us back to your bay area and told us to tell you goodbye for now and that we would meet you in Indianapolis. Dad, Mike, and I stood by your stretcher. I touched your arm and just told you we loved you very much, and we would meet you over there!! In my heart, I knew (as a nurse) that there was a very good possibility you wouldn't make it. Over and over in my mind I kept telling the Lord, "I don't understand. Why didn't you protect him?" The Lord whispered back, "Linda, I did. I kept his airway open."

The air transport crew whisked you away! I let people lead me outside to a car. Pastor Dave drove us to Indianapolis that night. It was an absolutely beautiful night – cool, clear, stars bright in the sky. Pastor Dave and Dad sat in the front. Michael sat in the back with me and held my hand. I cried; tears kept running out of me. I couldn't believe this was happening!!

In the distance, we could see the light of the helicopter flying low. I remember Jesus' words: He is with us always (Matthew 18:20b). I believe that He was in that helicopter with you, and He was in that car with us. God reminds us in Psalms 139:7-12 that we can "go nowhere from his sight." Praise God that he could see you when mom couldn't. After a while, Craig, we looked out to our left while on Interstate 70. We saw your helicopter flying low in the dark, clear night sky. Craig, it was a beautiful, cool, crisp spring night. The stars were out; it was a beautiful night for a ride. Craig, what I did was picture Jesus beside your stretcher with a hand on your shoulder supervising all that went on. He was the co-pilot too, beside your helicopter pilot, getting you to Indianapolis.

Craig, it's like time freezes, and every minute lasts an hour; every thought is focused on the situation. I think I even told Mike that this can't be happening, because God doesn't let anything happen that we can't handle. I thought God had made a mistake, because I couldn't handle all of this. Your heart beats fast and forcibly forever. The panic in your heart and soul is so heavy and unbelievable, as if your chest will explode. I kept reminding myself God is in control, because we are Christians, and we had asked God to make **all** the decisions. We were supposed to just walk through the process and see what He would do. It is hard to wait patiently. From God's Word (1 Corinthians 10:13), comes a promise: "No temptation (or burden) has overtaken you but such as is common to man; and God is faithful, who will not allow you to be tempted beyond what you are able (to bear), but with the temptation (or burden) will provide the way of escape also, so that you will be able to endure it."

When we got to the trauma center (70 miles away) around 12:20 a.m., you had been there 20 minutes or so already. A chaplain named Leah met us and took us to a side room to wait. It must have been a doctor's area: big pool table, chairs, loungers, and vending machines. It was sort of dingily lit. Being taken here was not a good sign. I stood, paced, and prayed. The neurosurgeon on call arrived and said he had put a probe into your brain to measure your intracranial pressure. It was good, and they were taking more x-rays. We were taken upstairs to the PICU (Pediatric Intensive Care Unit) waiting room to wait for your arrival. Time went by so slowly!! It was about 2:30 a.m. when a nurse and resident talked to us and asked more questions. We learned that on a coma scale of 0-15, you were a 5 or 6 when you arrived there. You had no responsiveness to verbal commands, but you were moving your arms and legs some. Your pupils were reactive and small. All of these were good signs. Craig, you were at 4 at our local hospital before you were transferred. According to the coma scale, anything 8 or less is a severe injury. We later learned that someone with a trauma coma scale of 4 has about a two percent chance of survival, and with a 5, about a four percent chance of survival.

The neurosurgeon told us the first five days are most critical for your brain due to swelling, and the most swelling occurs during the first three days. My heart had heard that prayer request there, so I started praying for God to take care of all that He had said while we listened to more.

Then we got to go in and see you. Craig, I couldn't believe all the machines around your bed and hooked to you:

tubes, wires, monitors. I heard the sound of the ventilator inhaling for you. You looked so relaxed, so at peace, as if you were sleeping. Your color and physical appearance were so improved from when we said our goodbyes. The air in your abdomen was even gone! You truly looked as if you were sleeping. You had one tiny abrasion on your temple, another on the inside of your upper chest, cuts on your left calf (one had two sutures, and another had one suture). Other than that you had no visible injuries. You had a neck collar on, because they weren't sure about your neck; they thought it might be fractured.

Standing at your bedside, holding onto the bedrail, I whispered a silent prayer. My back had bothered me so bad that Friday that you had had to help me get off the toilet that morning. Mike had to help me in and out of Pastor Dave's car during our trip over, and I had stood most of the time while waiting at both hospitals. The chairs and loveseats in the PICU waiting room were too soft, oversized, and uncomfortable, and my back was **so** strained that I needed to lie down. My heart whispered to God, "I need my back fixed because this is going to be a long ordeal," and before I could refocus on you it was as if a big, warm hand pressed against my lower back and drained away ALL the strain and pain. I felt myself able to stand relaxed, without pain. I knew He was in that room. My heart rejoiced knowing HE was there!! I thought to myself, "He can heal you that way too, Craig, if He chooses too."

Craig, this moment helped me so much! I later had someone look up the population of Indianapolis proper in an atlas and found it was over 740,000. What blessed me Craig was the fact that I, Linda Tegeler, a nobody in the eyes of the world, whispered a prayer silently to her God, and He answered before I could explain my need, because He knew <u>my</u> need before I uttered it completely. Praise God! He is so awesome, Craig. In Matthew 6:8, Jesus says "...your Father knows what you need before you ask."

16

On Sunday morning, Pastor Dave and Mike returned to the trauma center to get Dad to go home to get our car. Pastor Dave and Mike had left to go to Dave's parents' house in Indianapolis to sleep some. Your Dad and I stayed right there. I spent most of the night right beside your bed, touching you, praying, and telling God how much I loved you. Pastor Dave, Dad, and Mike saw you before they left that morning. You rested so peacefully.

There are so many wonderful doctors and nurses who told me a lot of things, answered all our questions, and listened to our concerns. They are so caring and never in a hurry. Your nurses work one-on-one, whether they work 8-hour or 12-hour shifts, constantly watching all your monitors, IVs, tubes, etc.(a lot I don't understand).

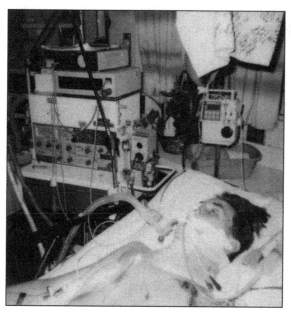

**Craig in PICU (Pediatric Intensive Care Unit)
on Day 8**

You have a lot of people praying for you. You were put on prayer chains throughout Wayne County. I was told later that someone had called TBN and someone told the Fussners in Indonesia. Craig, prayers were arriving in Heaven from all over the world, bringing Jesus your name and needs. God's word says He already knows, but He is pleased when the saints ask! I looked out over Indianapolis in the dark and saw all the lights in houses and the people represented by those lights in one big city. It is mind-boggling to know we can pray in the middle of all these people and God hears our prayers. Sometimes He responds immediately, and other times He waits. I believe you had angels nearby. Do you see them, Craig? God can give you spiritual eyes. Jesus is right here with you and me.

On Monday, your left lung collapsed. This didn't alarm or surprise me. Today, your face is so swollen that your eyes will hardly open, especially your right eye. Your upper chest, neck, and shoulders are puffy, supposedly from air being forced into your lungs with the ambu (a bag used to inflate the lungs when you can't breathe on your own) and respirator. When we press on the tissue around your neck and shoulders, the air pops and crackles. The upper part of your left arm to your elbow is swollen and bruised to a dark purple, but numerous x-rays show nothing.

The attempt to get your feeding tube in is unsuccessful. Your left chest tube is draining well, but you are coughing up bloody mucous in your ventilator tube. Your ICP (intra-cranial probe) pressure has been good!

It was mid to late morning. I walked into PICU to see you after Mike and Dad left to go home again. There were doctors and nurses all around your bed. My eyes saw the ICP probe number was at 31, so I left immediately and went to the lounge to call for prayer support. The doctors and nurses were on it and with you. I tried three times to call either the church or Bob and Ruth in Indianapolis, but the line was always busy. My heart was panic-stricken, but then that small still voice said, "Are you going to ask me?" I said, "Yes, Lord, I need his ICP number below 22, and they really want it below 20. Please lower it."

Before I could try the phone or decide what to do next, one of the nurses appeared, saying you were better. When I walked into the unit, I looked at the ICP probe monitor, and I watched it go down…24, 23, 22, 21, 20, 19, 18. It never went above 20 again. This was more reassurance; the Lord doesn't need a phone line! Just ask Him, because He's right there. The Lord hears those prayers we whisper, and He let me see Him answer it. My heart rejoiced again. The doctors and nurses could give no reason for the alarm or what spiked the ICP count. Jesus was in your room and took care of it.

Something unique happened this night. It was getting close to bedtime for you. We always had to leave PICU during certain hours, so the nursing staff could do some things. Your Dad was insisting I go sleep in a bed that night. I hadn't gotten a full night's sleep since Friday night and looked worn out. Craig, you had progressively gotten worse, and with your lung collapsing, I was afraid to leave. I thought you might die when I wasn't there! There were things your Dad didn't know because of my nursing skills, however outdated. I told your Dad I couldn't leave unless he could guarantee that you would be alive the next morning. Since I knew he couldn't do that, I knew I was staying, and he was not making me leave. No way! Then an elderly lady, a grandma who was there with her grandson in PICU, approached us and told me I needed to read Psalm 91:11. I told Dad we needed a Bible, so we walked to the lounge, found one, and read that verse. "For He will give His angels charge concerning you, to guard you in all your ways."

We returned to your room, Craig, and told the nurses where we would be if they needed us. We went across the skywalk to the motel and got a room. Craig, I pictured an angel on each corner of your bed-watching over you, your machines, and your nurse that night. I praise God that grandma had enough faith to obey and tell me what I needed to hear!! I hope I will be as obedient when God needs me to deliver a message to someone for Him.

We went to the motel next door, and a funny thing happened. It might not seem funny now, but either I was so tired I was silly or maybe the Lord knew I needed to laugh. I hadn't changed clothes since Saturday before your wreck. Some things aren't significant when it comes to life-and-death circumstances. Anyway, I took a bath, and it felt wonderful. I washed my bra and panties and let them dry overnight on the air vent. When I got ready to come out of the bathroom, Dad had all the lights on in the room, and there were sheers up to the windows. I asked him to close the curtains on either side of the sheers, but they were not made to close over the sheers. I asked him to turn off the lights, so no one would see me naked. He gently reminded me that we were on the seventh floor of a hotel and that we were up even higher than the hospital. There were no buildings close by and the only way for someone to see me naked would be for a helicopter pilot to hover outside our window with a pair of binoculars, and he doubted anyone was that desperate to see a naked woman. I laughed off and on for the next hour, jokingly keeping an eye out for any low-flying helicopters. By the time I had finished washing out my top and doing all the things a lady does in the bathroom, Dad had fallen asleep, and he never saw me!

It was so good to laugh at something ridiculous, when your life feels so fragile. I slept so soundly. When I finally woke up, your Dad was up, dressed, sitting at the table in the corner of our room by one of those big windows. He was writing checks to pay the bills at the church we attended. Life goes on for everyone else….Church life goes on, and the bills need to be paid. Dad was doing his part as treasurer for the kingdom, and I was focusing 100 percent of every waking hour on you.

Tuesday, May 24, 1994

Your other lung had collapsed during the night, and now you have another tube and jug. This really surprised me and was making your condition worsen. Today was to be the critical day for your ICP probe, but your damaged lungs were much more critical now. The doctors said your lungs are fragile little balloons, and the vents are having to use a lot of pressure to force the air into your lungs, because they are so bruised and full of blood clots and fluids. You look so unreal; your body is bruised, swollen, and attached to so many machines with wires and tubes going everywhere.

Wednesday, May 25, 1994

I had to go home to do some things and get some things! Craig, I had a dream about you. You were in a storm with lightning and rain. Two men were crawling across our yard, trying to kidnap you. I woke up fearful. It was 2:22 a.m. I had slept in your bed. I just laid there with your posters and stuff all around me. I cried and prayed a lot. At 3:40 a.m., I called Virginia, and we talked. At sunrise, your room was filled with rainbows from the prism in your window. Craig, God can make rainbows out of a ray of light, like He does after a thunderstorm using raindrops. The potential is always there; we can't see it until He reveals it at His precise time and when conditions are right. We have to endure the thunderstorm and its fury before the rainbows appear.

Dad stayed with you while I was home. Grandpa and Grandma came over to help me do some things. I had to do laundry and get things ready for Mike's graduation. Grandma ironed his graduation gown, and I tried to mail out some last-

21

minute party invitations, since Mike wouldn't hand any out at school. Several of the ladies from our Euchre Club came over with cleaning supplies and had the whole downstairs of our house cleaned, dusted, vacuumed, and windows cleaned for Michael's graduation and open house. I made a list and let them help me do it all in a couple hours, where it would have taken me a day or more to do it myself. Praise God for friends. I called them and asked for help; we shouldn't be afraid to do that when life throws us a curve ball. I told God I needed help getting things ready, and asked one of the ladies to help and she got the others. I was so blessed by all they did!! What can I say? I thought about you every minute. I called at 1:00 p.m., and you were having blood pressure problems. I believe God takes our heartache and agony and turns them into prayers.

"In the same way the Spirit also helps our weakness; for we do not know how to pray as we should, but the Spirit Himself intercedes for us with groanings too deep for words; And he who searches the heart knows what the mind of the Spirit is, because He intercedes for the saints according to the will of God. And we know God causes all things to work together for good to those who love God, to those who are called according to His purpose." (Romans 8:26-28)

Grandma and I ran to K-Mart to get some things–underwear for me and party supplies for Mike's graduation party. We saw Jan, a pastor's wife from another church in Fountain City, and she said they were praying for you. Right there in the K-Mart parking lot, we joined our hands. We asked God to take care of your blood pressure problems and to help the nurses get your feeding tube in (it still wasn't in after four days).

Yvonne brought me back to Indianapolis at 4:00 p.m. It's like you go through all the motions of life with some things still having to be done. I praise God for friends and family who help, lead, and are there! I keep wondering how the final chapter will read in your story.

Thursday, May 26, 1994

Craig, you have developed a sinus infection around your Miller Abbott feeding tube. You got your ICP probe out today! The nurses and doctors still can't get that feeding tube to pass from your stomach into the large intestine (through that little opening). Your blood pressure and lungs are all irregular today and you are being observed closely. Today, you will get an MRI; they think they can get all of your machines on the elevator. They want a clear picture of your neck and chest.

Craig, you have had three brain scans to my knowledge (one at our local hospital and two here). They have shown O_2 deprivation. One doctor even chastened me because I wasn't taking this seriously; Jill and Laura were visiting when he had given me the reading of the third scan done in PICU. I nodded to his report. Jill and Laura exchanged their concerned nurse looks to each other. Craig, sometimes God wants us to stand on what He has revealed to us in the secret places of our souls and believe it until He says No. God and I had talked and discussed a lot over the last six days. My most frequent question was "Why didn't you protect him?" God would whisper that He did, but He did it His way. He revealed that He had kept your airway open and that was how He chose to protect you. I gently reminded God they (the doctors) were telling me your brain scans had showed O_2 deprivation, and God reminded me to trust Him!

One doctor asked if you had vomited at the scene of the accident. I even called Yvonne because we had been told she sat with you in the field until the ambulance came. Yvonne reaffirmed you had not vomited and/or aspirated anything while she was with you, but you made gurgling sounds. She and Brenda stayed with you in the field, praying over you and for you. We learned that you were pitched out of the truck into the ditch, as the truck rolled three times. April stayed in the truck during the accident, and when she got out, she ran to the neighbor's home in the dark. It must have been horrifying for her to have been awake during all of that. Then she found you and thought you were dead. She ran with all her might to get help; it was quite a distance. The way I understand it, Yvonne had gone somewhere that night. While coming home she came down Whitewater Road instead of going her usual way. Then she saw the truck in the field with its lights on, and she went to get help, not knowing where you were in the field. The music was playing on the truck radio. Those two mothers sat there with you until the rescue workers arrived. Fountain City First Responders arrived first. Yvonne said your left arm was twisted backwards, and your left leg was underneath your body. You were making gurgly noises, but you had not vomited. I asked her to tell us her view of the accident.

5-3-98

Dear Linda,

I remember the night of Craig's accident as if it were yesterday. I have often wanted to write about that evening but never took the time.

I don't want to make this too dramatic, yet in my life- I knew this was directed by God. That is the only way I know how to describe the events that went on that night. I really don't want to sound as if I think I was some kind of hero; I was NOT! I was so afraid. When I realized that the truck in the field had been wrecked, I wanted to keep on driving but God moved me on.

I had been to visit Diane that Saturday evening late in May. At that time Don was Dee's Sunday School teacher. The class had taken an offering after the death of Caryn, their daughter. We had put off taking the money to them.

We had dreaded the visit because of the awful circumstances, but that afternoon I really felt it necessary that it be done that evening. I knew Don couldn't go that night, but I was going to go anyway. The visit wasn't anything like I thought it might be. How could money even begin to tell them how sorry we were? After I went, I was glad I had gone. The Lord had been there in our conversation and prayer.

I was on my way home, thinking about what we had said, the sorrow they were feeling, and the loss!!! I felt heavy-hearted and just wanted to get home to my own family. I was driving slowly up Whitewater Road, because they had been doing road work all week. Parts of the road had been covered with gravel. It was dusk and hard to see. I had just gone around the two sharp curves and was headed east up the hill, when I noticed a truck in the field on the left. At first I thought a farmer parked out there, yet a second look told me something wasn't right. I heard the thump-thump-thump from the radio, but no one was around. The dome light was on in the truck, the cab was crushed down on the driver's side, the back glass was broke, and the passenger door was open. The truck, pointing east...and many feet from the road...was an eerie sight. At first, I paused for just a moment to be sure no one was in the truck. There didn't seem to be anyone around, but I suddenly knew I better get help. I punched the accelerator and headed to the nearest home. I prayed up the road and in the driveway for God to be with them (whoever was involved). As soon as I got to the back steps of their house, I saw blood. It seemed to me like a lot of blood. I opened the door and yelled, "There's been an accident! Call 911." Brenda met me in the middle of the kitchen. The trail of blood led through the kitchen and into the front room where April was sitting on the couch with towels around her. Kara and Doug were trying to calm her down and stop the bleeding. She hadn't been there five minutes, because Brenda had just dialed 911 and was about to run back to the truck and look for Craig. I will never forget the words she said to me, as we were running out the back door and to my van. April said Craig was lying in the field, and she was afraid he was dead! My first words were, "He's not dead!"

As I was backing around the driveway, everything was becoming real. I was so scared, I didn't want to find Craig in that field. I didn't want any of this to be happening. I thought of Paul and Linda, especially Linda. We had been doing a Bible study on Spiritual Warfare and we had learned and shared a lot. This was her son out there, and the devil wasn't going to destroy him. From one mother's heart to another I had to do something. I started praying, I mean <u>really</u> praying. In the name of Jesus, let Craig live and not die! I was praying out loud. I don't remember all I prayed that night. I do remember praising God and calling Him our awesome Father. The teachings we had learned began to flood my mind. I was binding Satan and claiming healing. Suddenly, we were getting out of the van and running to the field.

It was completely dark now, but with the headlights, it wasn't difficult finding him. I was surprised I hadn't seen him when I was there earlier. I was very grateful to have Brenda with me, and I'm sure she was glad I was there too. Craig wasn't five feet from the road, at the very edge of the cornfield. I remember the actual position of his body, I kneeled down on his right side, and Brenda was on his left. We talked to him, telling him who we were and that help was coming. I softly touched his chest, leg, and arm, all the time praying. His eyes were open, but they rolled back occasionally; they were moving but not focused. I remember thinking of my own children and what would I want someone to be doing if it were them at the side of the road. Now, we were both praying. Brenda was so sweet, but both of us wishing someone would get there soon. When I prayed everything I knew to pray, I began to pray in my prayer language. The Lord really took over as I prayed and kept praying. His breathing was so labored, but his chest kept rising up and down. I wanted to straighten his right arm and leg, but I knew better. It seemed so dark and it was beginning to get cold. Where was help? Finally after what seemed like forever, we heard sirens a long way off. I was glad they were coming, but it was so strange to know they were coming to us. A police officer arrived first. He went to the van and got a T-shirt that Lucas had left in there from some baseball practice, and he covered Craig's chest with it. I remembered there was a blanket in the back, so he ran and got that. Why hadn't I thought of that? Actually, the officer didn't seem to be much help. He must have gone to the truck and turned the engine off or at least the radio. Funny, I never noticed the radio at all. Brenda had gotten up to speak to the officer. He had been questioning us about a lot of things, but I just prayed. Later, I tried to remember all I had said to the Lord and to Craig, but not much came back. One time, I remember praying, "Lord have your own way with Craig, he belongs to you." I remember praying for peace to be with (them) through everything, but I certainly didn't think about what lay ahead. I prayed for healing and wholeness, even though it seemed to be anything but those things.

When the ambulance arrived, everybody else did as well. The area rescue team was there and more people than I can remember. I do remember not wanting to leave Craig's side, but someone helped me up, and I looked only long enough to see them rip his shirt off. I had to look away. Brenda and I were standing in the field, leaning on each other. I thought for a moment I might just fall to the ground. We had our arms around each other and slowly *walked back to the van. By then, they were pulling away. I don't remember driving back to Brenda's, but people were helping April. Her parents had been called, but I don't remember thinking much about April. I went inside their house to see if you (Linda and Paul) had been contacted. I don't think anyone knew. Suddenly, a desire to go home just washed over me! Randy (from the Ft. City rescue squad) had turned my van around in the driveway. He offered to drive me home, but I thanked Brenda for being there and drove myself home.*

When I got home I was shaking. I told the family what had happened, and Don prayed for Craig, April, and their parents. It seemed good to let someone else pray awhile. Lizzie called Melissa and her mother and got the Baptists praying. Someone from church called to see if what they were hearing was true, but I just sat on the couch, covered up and wondered.

Kyna, the church youth leader, pulled in the driveway and asked if I wanted to go to the hospital with her. She had heard about it on the C.B. I felt so tired and could barely move from the couch, but Liz and I went. When we got to the hospital, we saw the helicopter on the landing pad. I remember Kyna saying "Oh my God! As we parked, I saw Pastor Dave opening the door of his car to help you in. Only then did I realize Craig was going to Indianapolis. I will never forget the look on your face, Linda. You looked like a little girl, so dazed it seemed they were just leading you along. I don't think we said anything, and again I prayed. We went inside the hospital. Lizzie was with Teddy. They went back to see April. Kyna, Marsha, Jill, Virginia, and I went to the chapel in the hospital. We prayed there for a long time. We knew the Holy Spirit was there.

The next morning, we drove to Indy, but we weren't allowed in to intensive care. We talked to you but I don't

*remember a lot about the visit. During the next weeks, we
made several trips to the hospital....*

God gently reminded me He had put prayer warriors at
your side, and He had put the people He wanted where they
were at the appointed time. I felt Dr. Craft was one of those
people He placed on that shift that night in the ER at home.
He had assembled the saints to pray! This is how He chose
to protect you. The Lord and I talked about this a lot, Craig,
as you will too later!!!

Craig, you had a lot of visitors today! Your face and eyes
are so swollen you have only slits for eyes. Darrell came to
see us, and he talked about Deanna's death from her tragic
auto accident, and said his trust in Jesus is stronger today
than before. I can't imagine that at this time, Craig. I hurt so
bad; I wonder how this will turn out. I never, ever thought
something this bad would happen to our family. Shock and
questions plague me about the sense of all of this!! I guess I
see this huge mountain of pain before me, and I don't want to
even begin to scale it!! I know we don't earn blessings, but I
really struggled with a lot of tough questions, Craig, and the
Lord will help me through most of them down the road.

Waiting on that MRI seems like forever, Craig. The
doctors wanted a closer look at your cervical spine, so they
can clear your neck of the cervical collar. There has been
a questionable area in your neck, and the MRI of the area
would give a definite answer to their concerns – whether or
not your neck is broken.

Craig, my apprehension mounts today. I am questioning
God on His promise in 1 Corinthians 10:13: "No temptation (or burden) has overtaken you but such as is common
to man; and God is faithful who will not allow you to be
tempted (burdened) beyond what you are able, but with the
temptation (burden) will provide the way of escape also, that
you may be able to endure it." I knew I couldn't handle all

of this. I hurt so bad. The pain was indescribable. I imagined the worst!! I'm supposed to praise God that you are alive and let Him take care of the rest, yet I wonder if you will live. Also, I wonder if you will you be mentally impaired, have a different personality, be able to walk/ feed yourself. Dad seems so positive. Why can't I be? Being a nurse makes it harder at times, yet "with God all things are possible" (Matthew 19:26).

They haven't been able to do your MRI because you had been too critical to move. Plus, the machines you need won't fit in the elevator. The portable x-rays of your chest and arm were done in PICU. I keep wondering what the verdict of your MRI would be and just committed it to the Lord. He is in charge of everything, even the timing of all things.

Craig, as we go along, I record some of the things I learn about what happened. As we put together the pieces, sometimes I don't hear things until days later, when someone visits, or we catch a doctor we hadn't seen for a while.

Friday, May 27, 1994

Today is Aunt Claudia's birthday. People from school, younger and older students, come to see you.

Dad and I had to go home for an awards program for Michael. Some of this is a blur! When we returned, one of your resident doctors greeted us and said your right lung had partially collapsed again. They can't seem to get it reinflated. When your pulmonary doctor met with us she just kept saying they had done all they knew to do; repositioning you a little, repositioning the tube, increasing suction. Nothing was working.

While she was showing us pictures on the PICU x-ray light screen, it was as if that small still voice said, "This is not of me." I let your doctor finish her explanation, and then I told Dad we needed to pray. We prayed, using biblical appropriations given to God's children, and asked that God's power be exhibited here, using Jesus' name and blood to claim healing. Craig, your lung was completely reinflated by morning. Praise to God!

Some of the school officials and one teacher came to see you today. They mainly looked. Your teacher and guidance counselor were very nice and friendly, offering help.

Today, we talked to your neurosurgeon. He said your brain stem was sort of twisted and tilted when your brain was jostled. The brain's wires were all pulled loose causing little bleeds (this type of injury is called shearing I think). Your brain was slammed against the front and back of your skull when you hit the ground. Your type of injury (and you have a couple) will take a long time to recover from. He said it will be four to six weeks before there will be 'any' response, and if you can then move a finger, that will be great. We will pray about this!

A father of one of your friend's is in very serious condition at home in the hospital. We will pray for Darrell and their family while we are here.

Craig, I love you so much. It hurts me so to see you lie so still and look so blank. I am writing this journal in response to a suggestion from one of the nurses of PICU. She asked me to tell her about you, so you wouldn't be just a head-injury patient to her. I started sharing things about you....

"Craig loved life."

"Craig loved to ride the scooter he had (he had a helmet and was safe with it)."

"Craig loved karate and had three belts already."

"Craig wanted to be a police officer."

"Craig had a girlfriend."

Then she gently reminded me that Craig is still here and said I was referring to you in the past tense. She told me to focus on today, buy a journal, and write your changes in it. That would help me see your progress and record what happened to you along the way. If you recover, she said, it would help you know where you had been and let you put the pieces together. She told us the Craig we knew might be different after the injury, but as long as you were alive, there was hope. I went to the gift shop, got a journal, and started writing this. I also bought a devotional, <u>My Utmost for His Highest</u>. I read this daily to seek what God had to say about each day. I posted a picture of you at the front of your unit so the staff could see the Craig I knew before the accident.

Craig on motor bike, a 16½ year old sophomore (the picture we put above his bed so the nurses would know the Craig we knew).

Craig, you were getting a lot of visitors in PICU. Your dad and I were asked if we wanted to limit visitors to just family members. We knew you had a big circle of friends, and we were told your friends could be a big part of your recovery later on. Your dad prayed about it, and I did too.

We agreed together to leave visitation open. We felt the Lord wanted people to come. We were warned there would be "spectators" as well as genuine friends, but we still agreed we had to leave it open. I knew you wouldn't be too happy we did this, but we felt we were supposed to at the time; we were being obedient to God. A wide variety of people came during your three-month stay. Some came only once to see you at your worst, but that was okay. Some friends held your hand, talked to you, cried, and showed you they cared. A lot of faithful friends and classmates made frequent trips, and I praised God for them. One day, I found a mother there with her two sons; she was giving them an object lesson in driving and how vehicles can result in terrible accidents. During that visit, I left and prayed, for she had no idea how that hurt. That mother was just being a mom, trying to protect her sons from a similar tragedy. Our friends came to give us hugs and words of encouragement. This made the days pass a little quicker and seem more bearable. Many of those people who came only once might not realize it but they saw a miracle in the beginning.

Craig, we have to obey even when it hurts; God can even use the ugly things of life for good if we let him. I have had groanings too deep for words. Romans 8:26-28 says: "In the same way the Spirit also helps our weaknesses; for we do not know how to pray as we should, but the Spirit Himself intercedes for us with groanings too deep for words; and He who searches the heart knows what the mind of the Spirit is, because He intercedes for the saints according to the Will of God."

Craig, I helped with your bath, and we washed your beautiful hair. The nurses are suggesting a trach, since it would be better for your mouth. It would get the vent tube out and give you more freedom to turn. There was an incident with one of the night nurses, I think. Your vent tube is pulling the corner of your mouth down, and saliva is pooling there. You are starting to get a sore. I told her we needed to work on this, or you will have a big open break at the corner of your mouth. She said it wasn't really going to matter (she thinks you aren't going to survive). Dad told her it did matter, and if she didn't want to take care of it, we would get someone who would. I just stood there and cried! Craig, it does matter! We prayed for that nurse. She cleaned the area and suctioned out the excess saliva. (Today, I can see the little scar, because I know where to look, but it isn't noticeable to anyone else. I wish she could see you now!)

This wasn't mentioned to hurt anyone in particular or place blame, but even those little things do matter. We should approach each patient as if everyone will survive; God can raise any one of them up as He pleases.

Today, you started your labored breathing they forewarned us about. The nurses adjusted your medicines. Your 30-80 respirations per minute are hard to watch. They predict you will sweat profusely and have this labored/abdominal breathing for two to three weeks. You could become agitated and possibly belligerent, indicating damage to those areas of the brain.

Every time they tell us a specific problem and/or expectation, we take it to the Lord, since He is the one ultimately in control. We ask Him specifically to take care of all these predictions. We have prayer warriors at home too. I call weekly, Craig, and give these specific requests to them! I am so anxious for your lungs to heal. We are asking the Lord to stabilize your lungs so your tubes can come out, and so you can come off the ventilator. I can hardly stand having to wait so long and not knowing how long this is going to last. Will it be six months or a year? Will you ever by okay again? I want so much to see you dressed for your prom or Young Explorers! You looked so good in your uniform. I **know** the Lord can raise you up, but will He? He healed Michael!

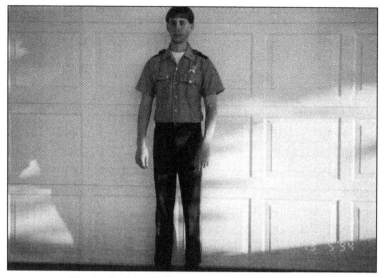

**Craig in his Young Explorers uniform
(a Sheriff law enforcement program).**

Michael's Healing Ten Years Earlier

Craig, you were little (5 years old) when Michael got an incurable disease that affected his central nervous system. Remember, Mike had seizures and loss of function in his left arm and leg for brief periods (paralysis). After weeks and oodles of tests, the doctors finally found the cause. Some of the details, the rarity of the disease, and no treatment options sent me to the Lord!! They even questioned if his intellectual process had been affected as well as his dexterity and coordination. Craig, God walked us through that two-year journey of surrender, growth, trust, and eventually his healing. God spoke it!!! Michael became an athlete and excelled in college – summa cum laude. We praised God for all He did in Michael's life and now yours. God has your life in His Hands.

Back to Craig:

Dad had to go back to work soon. Craig, it's going to be you and me climbing the mountain together. Maybe Jesus will pick us up and carry us both over. Have you seen Jesus yet? Jesus is real and if you need Him to show you where He is and the way out (of your coma), He will. Just pray, "Show me, Jesus." I want to understand it all, Craig. But I keep telling myself I don't have to understand: I just have to trust! Jesus gets to do everything! I don't think we have hit bottom yet; it scares me to think of what else can happen. Craig, we have an enemy that wants us to doubt the sovereignty of God in "our" lives or that God loves us. Satan knows my weak spots, and you are one of them. I love you so much!

Craig, standing beside your bed in PICU, it was quiet at night and I was playing some of your FCA tapes that Heidi, your FCA director, brought me. The nurses encouraged us to play music familiar to you. God painted a word picture for me using you, Craig. I was standing at your beside and just silently telling God how much I loved you and all the neat things about you. Your respirator was making that rhythmic sound as it inhaled and exhaled for you. Your body seemed so at peace, but I knew it was all broken. Your lungs were bruised and filled with clots and fluid, draining blood into your chest tubes and the bottles underneath your bed. Bruises are appearing now on your body several days after your wreck. My soul was in agony, Craig. I told the Lord how much I loved you, and God whispered, "I love him, too! Remember that Jesus, My Son, was broken for Craig. That's how much I love Craig and you." I wept, Craig!! We don't understand the magnitude of God's love. We sing about it, and we talk about it, but we don't really understand it. Can you imagine Jesus' mom standing at the front of her son's cross and watching her son being beaten and mocked? It hurt her as a mother. She was just a mom, too!!

Saturday, May 28, 1994 (at 4:20 a.m.)

Craig, I couldn't sleep. My stomach hurts. I can see you being rolled in that truck and being thrown out. I wonder how much you saw and about the terror you felt, how April felt, and the panic of it all. God is in control. I believe God was watching then and is now. He allowed it all to happen. I never imagined you would ever be hurt this way! I really felt God would protect you, but He kept your airway open. This question and a couple others will haunt us for quite awhile, but God is the only one who can give our souls rest. I seem to keep going over things in my mind and my heart. I have questions. You can't rest because of all the busyness and activity going on, but you are so tired you can't think straight. You have no desire for food; your whole focus is on the accident and what it has done, the seriousness of each thing, and there are so many.

Craig, we have a steep mountain to climb; Jesus promises to climb it with us. I pray in my heart I can climb it with you and be all you need me to be.

Craig, one night, we left and went to the Andersons to sleep. Your labored respirations (60-80 a minute) just seem to be so unnatural and tiring to watch. It hurts me that we can't stop any of this or do anything! But we can; we recommitted you to Him who is able to do the impossible. I had to envision Psalm 91:11 again, go to bed, and sleep.

Saturday, May 29, 1994

We called to see how your night was, and you had rested well. Your respirations were rapid but not out of control. Those angels must have helped!! Another resident went over your progress for the last seven days;

Your chest x-rays show improvement.
Your left chest tube went from suction to gravity
   – that is good.
Your feeding tube finally passed.
You're feeding on 75cc to 90cc.
Hype AL (a special IV nutrition until feeding tube
   went in) was discontinued!!
Off pain narcotic
O$_2$ on vent down to lowest at 32 percent.
Groin IV out.
Foley catheter out with special fitting so you still
   urinate into a bag, using a shield instead of a
   catheter.

Now our goals, Craig, for the next week:
Still need better x-rays to clarify if neck has cervical
   fracture, and get collar off if no fracture.
Tube feedings of 100+cc tolerated with resulting
   bowel movement.
Get chest tube out.
Clear intubation from mouth either on own or with
   trach, but likely by trach.
Just let you heal – your head, your chest.
2-3 weeks possible with rapid breathing and sweats
   – all from injury to different areas of brain.

This helps me see where we have come from and what
goals they have. It tells me how to pray and how to tell my
prayer warriors to pray. Craig, it has been a Very Long Week
(and only one week with many more to follow)!!!
   April, your girlfriend, came. I asked if she preferred you
shaved or rugged- looking, and she prefers you shaved. You
haven't been shaved because of your neck collar and of all
the tubes and wires, but we will try. Your eyes are a little open
and move some. You are off the narcotic and are on Versed,

a sedative/analgesic supposedly so you won't remember any of this. Several friends visited. You had a restful day, finally!! They changed your cervical collar, since they still are not sure of your neck. There is a small blister on your heel; that is not good!!

You had more visitors. Emily, your cousin, came. George and his son Chris came with Linda, his fiancée.

Oh Craig, how sad I am you are here and because of all that has happened. We are happy you are still alive and some things are better. I keep wondering if you will come back to us the same, Craig. My heart's desire is that you are healed miraculously to baffle all our family and doctors, glorifying God. But we might have to go through the whole nine yards to really speak to people. There are people out there telling your dad that they have prayed for you and God has just given them a peace. These people, Dorothy Fulks, Don Wine, June Austin, feel you will be restored. They prayed till God gave them His peace; now, they just wait with us.

Laura, your classmate, read her Bible for the first time in a year or so to get the verse for your T-shirt they are making you. Chris, another classmate, said he had not prayed for two years until he prayed for you, Craig. Show them, God, that you answer prayers.

George, a Christian friend from out of town, had a burden for you and us too, Craig, two weeks <u>before</u> your accident. The burden got so great they decided to drive over to see us and learn what was going on. On a Sunday night, they stopped in Fountain City at the church, but it was closed; our church had moved their services to the Friends Church north of Fountain City. They went to the services, not knowing what had happened to you. Your wreck had been on Saturday night, a day earlier. Ryan, your classmate and friend since probably kindergarten, was anointed in your place. The FCA concert had been changed to a prayer service.

Craig, there are others here in PICU who need our prayers. "Lord, be with the girl with the lacerated ear. Be with the teenage girl with the brain tumor and her family too, Lord. They hurt so badly too! Be with the girl with the amputated leg. Be with the little person who fell in the pool; his lungs are in need of healing too, Lord!"

Craig, you're having a CT scan of your head and neck. Dr. Lahaby is on tonight. Thank you, Lord!

Monday, May 30, 1994 – Memorial Day

We came early and had to wait to get in to see you. The nurses weren't done yet with your a.m. care.

My devotion challenged me to bank on my faith of who God is. Craig, God loves you so much. His son's body was pierced, bruised, and battered for your transgressions. You get to share in that suffering. Have you felt it yet? Jeannie, a friend from church, wrote us a letter and told us how the church is praying for you. This is bringing the church together as a family. It's too bad it takes a tragedy, but praise God He uses it for good. Many are praying all day long!!

They explained more medical stuff to us to help us understand. Your brain injury resulted when you were thrown through the air. First, your brain was slammed against the front of your skull. When you hit the ground, the brain was slammed against the back of the skull. While your brain was being jostled, the brain and brain stem were twisted slightly. The little wires to all the different areas of your brain were pulled loose. This is called shearing. (Craig, you had multiple shears.) Areas in your brain were bruised. One area was on your brain stem, and one was deep inside your brain. That CT scan on Sunday showed no more tilt to your brain. We didn't know it showed a tilt to start with; sometimes ignorance is a blessing!! Your chest sounds are better, and you are breathing on your own more. Craig, God can use His power to rewire your brain where it is sheared. They say we will know more when you wake up; they are backing off your Versed to let you wake up. They predict you will be agitated.

Your goals:
Chest tube out on Wednesday or so.
Get that cervical collar off.
Back off the vent – maybe a trach.
Dilantin off today.
(Craig, they thought you were having rhythmic movement like a seizure, which is common in a head injury, but they stopped it – they decided it was like a biting reflex to tubes in your mouth).
Less sedation to check neuro and your reactions.

They will be checking you to see if you open your eyes or flinch to pain. They are pinching you on your inner thighs to see if your react; you are getting bruises there.

I try to be positive (for people) that Craig will be whole again. I wonder a lot. Lord, forgive me. I think of all the different degrees of recovery – even the possibility of Craig staying the way he is right now. Lord, help my unbelief! Help me to commit, to trust, to surrender my will for yours, Lord! This is so easy to sing about, Lord, but it hurts so to live it. All of these words require a spiritual "action of faith" in the heart! We say we believe, but do we "believe with all our heart and soul?" Can we trust even when it results in a No? Help me to wait upon you, Lord. I used to think I wasn't one of Your special people. "No" really means it's not His plan or His way, Craig. We can think of a lot of "Yes" reasons or ways to glorify God and witness for Him. Help me to accept whatever Your will is for Craig!! Craig is Yours, not mine. (Psalm 34:3-7) says, "Everyone is special; God shows no partiality; He just blesses obedience; it will be His Way, His timing and maybe not even this side of Heaven."

Craig, you are receiving a lot of cards and letters. Through these cards and letters, people share verses and miracles in their lives. They are praying for you and for us. We read each card to you as it arrives, assuming you can hear us. One day, while I was reading your cards and letters, that still, small voice said, "Are you going to take my promise for you?" God had given us Isaiah 40:31 as Craig's promise: "Those who wait upon the Lord will gain new strength; They will mount up with wings like eagles, They will run and not get tired, They will walk and not become weary."

I said, "Okay, Lord, but I'm not sure how to claim this promise. What do I need to do?" I felt the Lord would show me how. We had a friend with a computer print this promise on an 8x11 sheet of paper and mount it on a sheet of royal blue construction paper. We put it with Craig's picture on the wall, at the head of his bed in PICU, and later in his room. (The prognosis throughout his stay didn't match what the verse said, but we chose the promise. It was up to God to bring the results).

We started taking pictures to go with Craig's journal. I borrowed a camera. The journaling and writing helped me pass some time, as well as record my thoughts and prayers. I felt so helpless and numb, but not hopeless!

Dr. Harvey gave us the x-ray results. They showed a "tiny chip" fracture of your skull, but no special problems or significance from it. Praise God!!

"Lord,

We have some prayers we need answers to –

We need to replace our vehicle that was wrecked with one that will meet Craig's needs in the future.

42

We might need a wheelchair; show Paul which one to get.

We need money for 1) the added medical expenses, 2) for Mike's college expenses, 3) for me while I'm in Indianapolis, and 4) for Mike's graduation gift and party.

We need a little time together as a family – before Mike leaves for college.

Amen.

Tuesday, May 31, 1994

Your neurosurgeon called me at Bob and Ruth's this morning. He said your neck collar can come off, because your neck is not broken. Praise God, Craig! Your MRI showed no significant damage from lack of oxygen. The swelling is receding. He said with your type of brain stem injury, it usually takes four to six weeks to come out of a coma. He said you would walk and talk again but to what degree would depend on you and God! He said Mom and Dad have to be patient. Our goal for this week was to decide about the trach; if you'll be able to do it yourself or if you will need a trach. Waiting for your MRI report seemed like an eternity. When I asked him about the O_2 deprivation, he said there was none! To me, Jesus autographed your MRI. There was no explanation other than it wasn't there! Praise God!!!! When I asked where it went, he couldn't say.

Craig, I constantly wonder how you'll be when you wake up. I wonder if your personality will be the same! Today's devotion challenges us to "put God first in trust." Secondly it says we are to "put God's needs first." God's needs will/ should be first, over ours. The Lord put His Father's will over

43

his own; we are to do the same. That's heavy stuff, Craig. The Lord did the Father's will. In the garden, when Jesus asked the cup to pass, the Father said no, and Jesus obeyed. Put God's trust first. God wants His Son to be manifested in my mortal flesh...in your mortal flesh. Will I be like a child and let Him mold me? Will I let Him mold you and gracefully watch as He does it His way?

Craig, PICU is full of rainbows. We brought your prism from your room at home and put it in the tiny window by your bed. The sun finally broke through and got the prism on the way up, filling your room with rainbows. It is absolutely beautiful!

Craig, we have two decisions to make. One is about where you will do your rehab. There are two pediatric rehab centers in Indiana, and both are in Indianapolis. One is at the trauma center and the other is in north Indy. Our insurance company wants us to check it out before we make a decision, cautioning us about the cap on our insurance which is $500,000.00. When it is used up, we will be on our own. We also have to decide about a trach to get you off the vent. They want to do it Wednesday or Friday? Lord, help us make decisions! Debbie and Cheryl are the two social workers who are helping us. They are making arrangements for us to visit the other rehab facility so we can decide. Rehab for head injuries is about two years. The first six months is the most rapid recovery, the next six months is pronounced recovery but not as rapid, and the second year you will see recovery. If there are deficiencies after two years, they usually remain, and there is usually some type of deficiency with every head injury. She's very positive and says some go on to lead normal lives, adjusting to their limitations. Where will you fit in, Craig? You were a wonderful young man before your wreck. You were sensitive to people's hurt. You were a disciplined person who worked hard at what was important to you: body building, guns, karate, target practice with guns and bows. You had oodles of fun and loved life. There I go again, referring to you in the past tense! I wonder who you will be at the end of this journey.

God, I keep thinking of James 1:5: "But if any of you lack wisdom, let him ask of God, who gives to all generously and without reproach, and it will be given to him." Boy, do we need some wisdom. I am so emotionally fearful of all the what-ifs, wondering what your future will hold. I would never love you less, because you aren't the Craig I picture. The world would, though? We need to make some decisions here, and we want God's will. God, you know Craig's needs and what would be best for Craig. You can control the estimates and guide the decisions. Lord, I prefer the trauma center!! Make it clear, so we will know.

Craig, I have so many questions for God! I get weary; the mountain still looms ahead and seems SO BIG.

Your chest tube on the left is coming out. The right chest tube went to water seal. The doctors are deciding on your trach.

Mike's graduation is coming up! I feel overwhelmed, and I have a lot of questions for Our Father. Even if you were going a little fast on that gravel road, you weren't doing anything stupid. It was your inexperience, the road repairs being done, and then when you started sliding, you overcorrected and rolled. That type of truck rolls easy. God chose not to spare you from injuries. People, even drunk drivers, walk away from wrecks every day, so why not you? I even believe God could have caught that truck in mid air and set it upright if He chose to, but He didn't. My heart hurts, because He didn't spare you all this. Over the next several months, you and I will wrestle with this question. It's okay. God can handle those questions, and He helps us grow through them.

Deb, the social worker, says I need a friend to talk to and share the hurt and struggles that lie ahead. Supposedly eighty percent of all couples who go through something traumatic like this get a divorce. The stress, the separation, the financial burdens, etc. take their toll on the marriage and family. I told her we were Christians. We have Jesus to lean on, and He would make the difference. My heart missed Paul and Mike so bad, and I wondered how long we would be separated.

"Lord, my flesh and my soul is in agony." I keep telling myself 1 Corinthian 10:13 is your promise. I feel like You have given me more than I can carry. I keep telling myself You love Craig more than I do. I can't fathom that yet. I know you sent your Son to die for mine. I know You can raise people from the dead. I know there are times when You say <u>No</u>. Help me to trust You with this hour...this day. God does not lie.

Craig, they are backing you off some of your medications. You squinted your eyes today, and your eyes teared when they suctioned you. Praise God !!

Craig, I read the scriptures about Elisha and how he was afraid. God opened his spiritual eyes so he could see and maybe God will do that for us. God does not want me to be afraid. He promises power, love, and a sound mind. 2 Timothy 1:7 says, "For God has not given us a spirit of timidity, but of power and love and discipline." God wants to walk us through this by faith, not sight, and faith comes by hearing the word (Romans 10:17). We read scriptures every day. We need to hear from God daily.

Craig, you had another scary episode tonight. Your dad and I had just gotten to Bob and Ruth's when something happened. Dr. Williams had the nurse call. Your blood pressure went up, your O_2 concentration went down, and your respirations became rapid again, so they reinserted your Foley, increased your medications, reattached your chest tube to suction, and increased your O_2. Your dad and I prayed with Bob and Ruth and entrusted you to God AGAIN! By midnight you were stable again. Dr. Williams couldn't explain what happened (but I knew God took care of it). Craig, sometimes the enemy of our souls taunts us, but what he intends for evil God can use for good. If God is for Craig, who can be against him? God is the one who will ultimately heal your brain or choose not to. God already knows the outcome of all this. Either way, God is still God. A no doesn't mean He loves us more or less. He loves us regardless of the outcome. "Lord, stop my doubt and questions."

Craig, I used to be the type of person who saw the glass as half empty. God keeps reminding me to see the glass half full – to count my blessings and see the positives. When I couldn't see any positives to praise Him for, I asked Him to help me, to show me something; He'd whisper, " Craig made it through another night," and I'd say, "Thank you!!" Praise God! Your lungs are better. Praise God your left chest tube is out. Praise God for your last IV. Praise God you responded to nasal suction and squinted your eyes. Praise God your neck collar is finally off.

Craig, I have all day to think and ponder and wonder. I wonder if we are pawns – maybe instruments for God to use to speak to others. Are we puppets? God doesn't really sacrifice one Christian to speak to those around Him, does HE? We either believe God or we don't. We can't trust Him one day and not the next. Our trust can't be conditional; we can't accept the blessings and reject the trials, tests, and tragedies. God wants to be Lord of everything in our lives. Help me to trust you, God, with today. Today, Craig, my heart is in agony again. I'm not sure how to let God be Lord over my heartache and agony. I miss Paul so much. I can't imagine being separated for three-four months. Can God be Lord over that too?

It was late afternoon, Craig. I was sitting in a rocking chair, resting and looking at the parking garage. My soul is in torment over questions of life. Then I thought I should just kill myself by jumping off the roof of the parking garage, because this is too much. I knew that thought had been put there by Mr. Liar himself! I knew that thought was displeasing to the Lord and chose not to consider it. Things might be bad, but God is in control. I have to choose to believe He can walk me through all of this waiting, emotional hurt, doubt, questions, all of it.

Craig, it's 7:30 p.m. I am waiting on Dad to arrive. I miss him and our family being together. If the Lord is my comfort, where do I find Him? I'm not sure where to start reading in the Bible. I feel emotionally, spiritually, and physically weak tonight. I can't concentrate or even quote scriptures. The Lord knows and understands.

Wednesday, June 1

Craig, Dad stayed with you today because I have to go home and get things ready for Michael's graduation.

Your dad had a hard time watching you lie lifeless there, as the therapists put you through their routines. Your eyes opened some. Dad read you six cards today.

Dad wanted to crawl into your body and take your place. Dad fasted for you, and he gave you to the Lord again. Your neurosurgeon told Dad you would have some permanent problems. We know God can do the impossible, and doctors can't. Dad said you moved your arms and your eyes a lot.

Thursday, June 2

Dad came home to go to Michael's senior awards program. Aunt Claudia and Grandma came to stay with you. Michael got several awards: a Precalculus award for most improved, the Citizenship Award, the Classroom Teachers' scholarship with LeeAnn, and an academic diploma. We are very proud of him, and we are very proud of you. April gave us a hug. A lot of your friends were there.

Dad took me to Fairview to clean out my desk; school will be out soon, and I'm not sure if I'll return to work as an aide there next school year.

Craig, we are having you anointed today at 5:00 p.m. James 5:13-16 says: "Is anyone among you suffering? Then he must pray. Is anyone cheerful? He is to sing praises. Is anyone among you sick? Then he must call for the elders of the church and they are to pray over him, anointing him with oil in the name of the Lord; and the prayer offered in faith will restore the one who is sick, and the Lord will raise him up, and if he has committed sins, they will be forgiven him. Therefore, confess your sins to one another so that you may be healed. The effective prayer of a righteous man can accomplish much."

Craig, while you are in PICU, we hear all the prognoses and see the huge mountain before us. Craig, I even heard Satan laugh and say "He got you." Your Dad and I decided to have you anointed. James 5:13 tells us to do that. We had Michael anointed! We are going to have Pastor Dave and Jill and Pastor Bob and Ruth do this, Craig. Remember Abraham and how he took his son to the top of the mountain. He even chopped wood for the fire. His son was awake but you aren't. God gave you to us to love, and we have. It's really up to Him to determine the outcome. Craig, we have to put you on the altar and leave you there, for God to do as He sees fit…what fits into His plan for your life. And then we have to watch and wait. Abraham got to take his son home. The hard part for us is waiting to see how all of this works out!! Pastor Dave's daughter Kirsten even came. Her eyes were big when she saw all the machines hooked to you. The nurses backed off for a brief period of time, so we could do this with some privacy. Other families watched from their bay areas!! I wondered what God will do!! Craig, I had to keep putting you back on that altar. I had taken ahold of you again, and God reminded me you belonged to Him. I had to let go and put you back up there on that altar. But who better to give you to than your Heavenly Father – Who can do the impossible!! I love you so much, but we have to give you up to Him! We asked God for His will, not ours. I said that with trembling knees, Craig, but we had to say it, do it, and believe it. We trusted Him to do what's best, and we believed He could do the impossible. We literally gave you to Him for His Will and His Purpose.

I remind myself that Jesus in you is greater than anything. He can lead you out of the darkness you are in.

Friday, June 3

We took our tour of the other rehab facility. When we arrived back to PICU the trauma doctor was already doing your trach. I personally am not feeling well physically; I must have not looked too well, because the nurse asked me what was wrong. I felt like I was getting a bladder or kidney infection. The doctors and nurses are so caring for everyone. They gave me the pharmacy number and had me call my family doctor to get a script to the hospital before the weekend. The staff warned us to eat, drink, rest, and take care of ourselves. We could not get sick. That wouldn't be good for us or you. I would have to work on this! You just don't think about food and drink in a crisis, but you still have to practice the simple basics of life.

Your trach was performed by the trauma surgeon. It wasn't a real neat trach, and the hole was too big for the canula. I was upset it wasn't done better, but we prayed for it, and it served its purpose – to get you off the vent so they could get you into rehab. Your mouth is clear now for better oral hygiene. We are trusting this trach to be very, very temporary!!

God engineered the timing of the last day or so. We wanted you anointed before the trach, and we wanted to be there when they did it, yet we needed to visit the other rehab facility and be there for Mike at his awards program. God took control and it all fell together wonderfully!

It is a daily battle for me, Craig, not to doubt or fear that you won't make it and if you do, will it be a 100 percent recovery? God wants us to trust Him daily to supply our needs – mine, too – and not worry about the future because He's in charge of it all, too! We must remember our song, "The battle belongs to the Lord." I play this song, plus several others, **every** day while we are with you during the daylight hours.

The staff is sharing at times what they think your deficiencies will be – where you appear to be injured. I will start watching too, so I can mark your areas and pray for them one by one. Craig, I doubt my emotional ability to do and be all you need me to be, but Philippians 4:13 says: "I can do all things through Him who strengthens me." Philippians 4:19 says: "My God shall supply all your needs according to His riches in Christ Jesus."

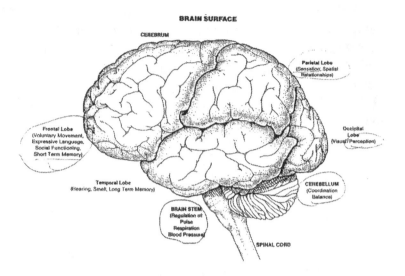

**The areas of the brain and their function
taken from Parent Notebook from the hospital;
the ones circled show areas where Craig had
involvement and where God healed.**

Craig, I feel we are in a spiritual battle here. Satan doesn't want you healed, because God would get all the glory. Your enemy, our enemy, will make it hard, long, and difficult - resisting us all the way. Remember who is greater here (1 John 4:4).

Craig, my heart is humbled by all the people who have reached out to us. You are a very special person, and I praise God for our family, our friends, our Christian brothers and sisters who share their resources, their time, and their prayers for you and us. God uses people to meet our needs!!

Saturday, June 4

Your right chest tube is out and you're moving out of PICU. Mike graduates today, and you did, too! Before they could get you situated in your bed, you had three bowel movements. Turning you from side to side to clean and change your bed, you started coughing with your trach, and bloody mucous went everywhere – in my hair, the bed, all over our clothes. Your arms and legs just flopped; you are limp all over. You look like a giant baby in a diaper, but you were worse off than a baby – you couldn't cry, eat, or move your arms. It hurt me so bad to see you that way; I just broke down and cried like a baby for you.

Phil and Virginia came to stay with you part of the day, so we could come home for Michael's graduation. Phil cried and wept when he saw you. Phil loves you, and it hurts him to see you this way.

On the way home, we prayed God will give us His grace to walk through Michael's graduation with joy in our hearts and smiles on our faces.

Michael was asked by his class to offer a prayer. He made it sweet and simple, asking God to get us through. There was even an article in the paper about it. Michael was FCA president, and his class wanted him to lead a prayer during the ceremony, but the administration said no. One of the speakers worked Mike in before his speech, and several cheered. God, you are present whether people invite You or not, and I praise God for that truth.

Craig, try to imagine Heaven with all the prayers arriving day and night; Jesus probably smiles and says, "That Craig has a lot of family and friends praying." People came and sat with you, Craig, and I appreciated that so much. Debbie, April, and Steve stayed until the afternoon on Sunday while we had Michael's reception. Then Jan and Darlene stayed with you a while too.

When we got back to Indianapolis around 7:00 p.m., you had had a blood culture because you had spiked a fever and developed an eye infection.

53

We read you your verse and prayed it with you as we had every night since God had given it to us (Isaiah 40:31). Craig, you have truly stumbled, and you are so weak; we want you to fly again, to walk and not be weary. Our devotion, Craig, says we have to trust and submit to His will.

Craig, it's sort of ironic. My back bothered me at home during Michael's graduation weekend, but when I get back to Indianapolis, it's totally okay. God's grace is sufficient, and He will meet all our needs.

Your physical therapist is a Christian, and she asked if you are, Craig. See, God has placed His people along the way.

You have rainbows in your room, Craig. Michael read you Chapter 8 in Mathew. It is so good to have my two sons together – however briefly. My heart weeps in gladness. You are moving your arms; your eyes are open more. You got a taste of chocolate ice cream on your tongue. You even yawned!

When I kissed you goodnight, Craig, your eyes got really big, and you just stared at me. Your silence is haunting, but we prayed, and I told you that "greater is He that is in you than he that is in the world." Jesus is greater, and He lives in you. I believe that, and I want you to believe that. We pray your verse. It is so hard to leave you alone, but you aren't really alone, are you (Psalm 91:11 and Matthew 28:30)!

The student nurses are taking turns with you as their patient. They all need experience with feeding tubes, trach care, positioning of comatose patients! You'll either shoot me or forgive me for this!

Tuesday, June 7

You flinched for the neurosurgeon, when he pinched you, and he was pleased. The neuropsychologist spent time with me, sharing about your type of brain injury and the prognosis. I was so upset; I cried through all of it. It was not positive. Then I told her who Craig was: your dreams, about your zest for life, your karate ability and belts, your friends. She shared about school, the difficulties you would have, possible gait problems, social disinhibition, attention problems, and that you would always need adult supervision; she indicated you would probably never be self-supporting.

Then it was my turn again. I told her about all your skills and abilities, as well as your dream to be a police officer. I told her you had recently joined the local sheriff's club and had attended their summer camp. I shared how you were a people-person, a peer helper (at school) who talked to other kids about their problems, and someone who loved life and lived it to the fullest. I told her you were a Christian, and our God would get us through this. I told her about your hunting and marksmanship skills. I even told her you were a neat-nut, probably the cleanest kid around with all the showers you took; you cared about being clean, neat, and well groomed. She listened to me. I told Dad about our talk, and he reminded me what God's saints felt after they prayed! We need to encourage each other and to remind each other to keep our focus on the Lord.

Craig, the insurance company and the hospital made a financial agreement, so we could stay here. Thank you, Lord; that was my heart's desire!

We moved you to your new room on the rehab unit. We decorate your room with your posters and your cards. We read each one again and show it to you before we put it up. We put your verse from God on the wall at the head of your bed with your picture.

You weighed 116.5 pounds. You've lost 25 pounds of muscle and tone. Therapies will be twice a day, every morning and every afternoon – physical, speech, and occupational. Time for each will be up to 45 minutes, as your endurance builds. Rest will be of the utmost importance between sessions and at night.

Our devotion in <u>Utmost for His Highest</u> says we are to cut the moorings loose and go out in the deep with the Lord. Craig, I hate deep water. The oceans scare me to death because I can't swim. We must try; it says we must act, and then we will know more. I'm not sure what the Word is telling us; we must move out into the deep, scary depths of faith…and therapies…and wait to know more.

Your friends keep coming!! Aunt Sylvia was touching and talking to you, and you cried a tear. Did you feel her love and sadness? It is wonderful to see you smile at your friends…and cry too.

Your first few therapies are in your room. You are so tired that you sleep through your bath and even part of your therapies – all typical of your type of injury. For me, it is emotionally draining. They are thinking your right side is weaker or more affected; we will pray about that, too.

Your rehab doctor; there is a big, fancy word for that which I can't say or spell, shared her expectations of your future. We will have to wait and see. I believe God can rewire the most damaged brain.

We need to pray for Anthony and his leg and Max and Cindy. In Mark 2, two men carry their friend to Jesus on a cot and let him down through the ceiling to Jesus, who heals him. We can carry Anthony to Jesus, and I carry you to Him every day.

Craig, when your friends come to visit, you smile and almost laugh. Everyone tells me how much you have improved!! They can see a big difference from one visit to the next. Teddy suctioned your trach. I am so thankful for all of your friends, especially the ones who can handle all the medical stuff and keep coming back.

Craig, I have to daily commit you to the Lord. I am not to worry or be anxious or fearful – that takes an act of mentally saying "no." I won't do that – you are Jesus' responsibility and burden. I am to love you, encourage you, and remind you who you are in Christ. Jesus in you is greater than anything. He can encourage you too. My heart's desire (Psalm 37:4-7) is the Craig Tegeler I know and his friends know will return and that you will have a new compassion and understanding of "life," telling others how Jesus led you out of the dark tunnel.

Praise God for Craig, his friends, family, and Craig's smiles/laughs tonight.

Pray for Francis, Darrell, Doug, Owen, and Chelly at college and traveling.

Trust in the Lord, and do good; Dwell in the land and cultivate faithfulness; Delight yourself in the Lord; And He will give you the desires of your heart. Commit your way to the Lord; Trust also in Him, and He will do it....Rest in the Lord and wait patiently for Him" (Psalm 37:3-7).

Friday, June 10

This is the first day you went down to therapy in your cardiac rehab chair. They lifted you out onto a big padded table the size of a ping pong table, only about a knee's distance off the floor. They are going to try to sit you up, and then roll you up to a standing position. Since you have your feet weighted with your casts, you are awkward to roll around. It takes about six people, but they dangle your feet over the edge of the table. There is a person at your back, one on each side, and one at your feet holding them flat on the floor. Then someone places a huge ball in front of you. They lay you across it and roll it till you are over it. You have no control, no strength. We do this a couple times. Then with you just sitting there, we help support you and hold your head up. I put a couple of my fingers on your forehead and a couple on your posterior head, and we raise your head so you can look straight ahead. I let go, and your chin hits your chest, like a limp rag doll. We do that several times. Supposedly we are retelling your brain to sit up, to hold your head up, and to stand up by doing these exercises. You are so lifeless. "This is going to take a long time," I realize. I was just beginning to comprehend what everyone had been trying to tell me. Craig was going to have to relearn everything – absolutely <u>everything</u>. I felt totally overwhelmed. No wonder it takes two years to recover from a head injury! This was only physical therapy. I was shocked even more when I began to see the deficit in speech therapy. When Craig couldn't point to a cat at the therapist's request, my heart sank. Later, as his therapies progressed, he could point to a cat, but he couldn't spell it. I realized the levels he had to climb. I sat and watched in awe, and I prayed like I've never prayed before. My heart prayed when I was too weary to utter a sound. My prayer warriors received my requests, and God heard our prayers.

Every two weeks, all the therapists from each facet of your care and rehab would measure your abilities or deficits with their own special sets of tests and come to a roundtable discussion to share your progress, assess goals for the next two weeks, and address your needs. The very first roundtable had me in tears. Craig was so "profound" in some areas that he couldn't even be measured. They assured me this happens to everyone and Craig will make progress. They also cautioned me that recovery might go faster in one area and slower in another. They originally told us your in-house extensive rehab would be 15-16 weeks with outpatient sessions after discharge that could go one to two years. His three therapies were twice a day and once on Saturday mornings. Saturday afternoons and Sundays were for rest.

I continued to do my part every day; we read from the Bible and played your Christian tapes. I just loved you!!! We watched TV, VCR tapes, wrote letters, and journaled.

Craig, you couldn't talk for quite a while, so I got to rule the conversations with no interruptions or arguments.

One day in particular I arrived after your morning therapies. Craig, you had this look of fear, panic, and concern on your face. You couldn't talk. You couldn't move your arms or legs to communicate, but you could nod yes or no. The Holy Spirit told me something was wrong. I whispered a little prayer that God would help me help Craig. I tried to remain calm and not cry. I asked you, "Craig, is something wrong?" You nodded yes. I asked if you were hurting anywhere. I think you said yes, and we went over the body parts until we narrowed it down to a headache. I asked you if you were afraid; you said yes. I talked and you listened. We went through what had happened and why you were in the hospital. I said you didn't need to be fearful. I talked about why you couldn't move your arms and legs, but that was only temporary, and we were exercising you to help you use them again. We talked about not being able to talk, but speech therapy was helping you learn to do that again. We talked about your feeding tube. That was how you'd eat now. You were wearing a diaper but wouldn't need one later. The fear and panic in your face left. I praise God I knew how to help you and answer some of your unspoken questions.

When you got more mobile, we explore the hospital in your wheelchair. We were on the third floor, so we ventured off to the gift shop, the cafeteria, the enclosed basketball courts with picnic tables, or outside the front visitors' entrance with circular driveway and lots of grass. It was June and warm; we'd watch for airplanes, cars, and people going and coming. I would wonder why these people were there, who they were visiting, and how things were going in their lives. The other families on the unit became your family there; we encouraged and helped each other.

It seemed we would be there forever. I asked God to send someone who had been where I was. Deb, the social worker, knew I was discouraged and had been crying. She introduced me to Christy who was going to be leaving soon with her teenage son. He had been in an auto accident and suffered some broken bones and a head injury also. Christy was a Christian. I remember her coming down the hall carrying her Bible. God knew before I asked, and He had the answer on the way (2 Corinthians 1:4). God comforts us in all our affliction so that we may be able to comfort others. Christy and I talked every day till she left, and we even saw each other when she returned for doctor appointments throughout the summer. Christy encouraged me to read the Bible first and the head injury notebook second. I read both and tried to keep my focus on the Lord.

We read in Matthew today that Jesus healed a little girl. My heart and soul aches daily for you, and I wonder if God will heal you. I love you so much. I tell myself this is all temporary, that God is able (in spite of what they say the future holds) and that we must do as your verse says: wait. The Lord keeps impressing this upon me: "those who wait upon the Lord."

Saturday, June 11

Dad's coming today. When Dad arrived, you were up in your rehab chair, and you showed off for Dad. You squeezed my left hand. You stuck out your tongue on request. We asked you to squeeze Dad's right hand hard; you beared down hard and bit your lips together straining. Praise God! Your Dad's voice broke, when he praised you for it. Dad and I went out to eat. Dad is staying with you on Sunday.

I got to teach Children's Church Sunday. I told them about you and how the prayers of Christians arrived in Heaven the night you were hurt and often since then. We went outside on the lawn and used strings to represent prayers reaching up to Heaven from everywhere. The center point was Heaven with

Jesus at the right hand of the Father. Matthew said it was the best prayer illustration he had even seen, but I think it was because they knew you, Craig, and it became personal.

Then I talked to the teens; some of your friends and classmates were there. It was silent: They listened as I cried and told them we didn't know what your future held, but we knew God loved you. He had been there that night and the last couple of weeks. He loved you more than I did, and that He was in control. I challenged them to walk closely with the Lord; we never know when or how we will need Him.

Aunt Claudia stayed with you Sunday afternoon and evening, and Dad came home. I have to stay over for a doctor's appointment on Monday and will see you Monday afternoon.

Tuesday, June 14

Today is Parent Education Day. Virginia came over and spent the day with me as your future caregiver. We attended therapies together and had a parent talk with the neuropsychologist. She compared the brain to a pan of jello. When you drop the pan hard, a lot of tiny hairline cracks appear throughout it. Those cracks interrupt the messages and signals sent through the brain.

We talked a lot about the insensitive things people do, unaware of how they hurt or the emotional damage done. I experienced several of these, Craig, and they are harder to deal with than your injuries. We shared some of our hurts and let them go. We talked about the spectators who come and the friends who stay faithful, yet even they must move on with their lives and activities. We talked about the rumors or details of the accident and the hurts they can inflict. That happened to your aunt. Someone saw your two leg casts and ASSUMED you had two broken legs, and passed that on to everyone. Aunt Sylvia called me crying and said she had just found out you had two broken legs; I reminded her she needs to question everything she doesn't hear from me. I explained the purpose of the casts: to keep your feet and ankles with a good angle of flexion so when you got ready to stand and walk, your muscles wouldn't be out of range. This is a good example of how gossip hurts, that person assumed casts meant broken legs and passed it on as such.

One mother used Craig as an object lesson for driving while drinking and speeding. I excused myself from that visit and went to the lounge and prayed. For once, I was glad Craig was in his coma!! There were other things over the course of Craig's recovery I had to overlook; most of it is ignorance or people's insensitivities. I just pray I never do it to someone else. If I have, Father, forgive me, because it truly hurts, and the sting lingers in your heart. Two mothers came crying to me of things said about their child. You can only comfort each other and move on, because the offending party usually has no idea what they have said or done or how it affected you.

We were encouraged to change our goals, to let go of our dreams for our kids in rehab. I listened and remembered who my God is; He made Craig with his gifts and talents; He can restore Craig or raise him up to be what He wants you to be.

We learned during the roundtable Craig had been out of his coma one week. Even though you still couldn't talk, you responded to commands and were aware of your surroundings. Praise God!!! Your projected date for discharge is mid-September. Your wreck was four weeks ago and you've been out of the coma for one week, so you are doing a lot more than they expected. They casually mention you will need braces to correct anticipated gait problems.

Today, Craig, you were able to pick up your baseball cap and put it on twice. I cried as I watched you. It wasn't smooth and quick; it was work to do something so simple, but

I praise God that you accomplished it. Oh! What we take for granted!! You even helped put your shirt on. God is in charge of all your rehab. Craig – your recovery is His burden. I just get to watch from a box seat. Craig, you said "Mom" today during speech therapy, when Char plugged your trach. The first time you mouthed the word Mom, no sound came out. She told you to try again – take a breath and force it out your mouth. "Mom" came out loud and clear. It was absolutely wonderful; you smiled big, and I cried. It was so wonderful to hear your voice again. As I sit rewriting this, I'm crying. I remember this moment so well. It was wonderful seeing Craig emerge again after all those days of silence and pain and ugliness.

You ate a little ice cream today, and you got your first drink from a straw. You choked and coughed some, but you had good sucking power.

You weren't sure if your vision was blurry, when we asked you. You recognized the words "hat" and "ball", but you couldn't recognize "sun" or "water".

Craig, your girlfriend came today with her friend and their moms. You were so glad to see everyone. You used your index finger to motion to your girlfriend to come to you. You must remember who she is and her specialness to you. Sometimes I marvel at what I see you remember or recognize. At other times, you are blank. You tried to mouth something when they left, but we couldn't understand what it was.

The therapists and social workers have shared how it is hard for some teens and even family members, immediate and extended, to accept the reality of a TBI and all it means – the long recovery, the probable changes that happen and those that will be necessary. They keep indicating life for us will **never** be the same.

At 7:30 p.m. Craig, you just swung your heavy, casted leg over the bedrail like you were going to jump right out of bed. Oh no, I thought, you are getting agitated like they said you would. Then you urinated in your diaper and indicated to me you had by pointing to your diaper area. Your awareness is so much better, I wish you could talk. Silence can be deafening as well as frustrating, yet I am thrilled at your progress. You now know when you have to go to the bathroom to urinate.

"Lord, keep my eyes and heart and mind focused on You, and let me trust You and Your final verdict which is still out for us earthly beings, but You know how this will all turn out."

Craig, your dad thinks I pick at you – fussing over you, touching you, holding your hand. I even put my hand on you while you rest. I am just trying to encourage you, help you, and stimulate every inch of you to help you be Craig again.

Friday, June 17

Craig, you climbed out of bed last night so now you have to have a Posey restraint jacket on when unattended. You seem very somber or mad. You stood up three times in physical therapy. You need to work on upper body and arm strength. You urinated in the urinal for us. You know when your bladder is full. Communication is a real problem; it is not easy for you to relay your needs and questions.

You wretched during your tube feeding. It scared me to death. With your Posey jacket on, I couldn't get you rolled over on your side if you vomited. You seem tired or less alert today. Your smile is so precious; I wonder what you are thinking when you smile.

Christy's son Adam goes home today! Praise God! Dustin is a little guy who has cerebral palsy; he had surgery to walk better and is in rehab here with you. He likes to spend time in your room, Craig! He is so cute and precious! Help him too, Lord!

Saturday, June 18

Please have mercy on us, Lord! Craig, you are so sober and lonely looking. You did not smile today! I don't know what to do or say. You aren't even telling me when you need to use the urinal. It breaks my heart to see you so down and discouraged. We watched three movies. I'm not sure you were even watching them. We played our music and read the Bible like we do every day. Pastor Bob and Ruth came, saw you, and prayed with us.

We went to the gift shop and got your dad a Father's Day card and gift (a candy bar and cookie – due to limited finances and limited selection in a hospital gift shop). Craig, you tried to sign the card, but you didn't have enough strength to hold the pen tight enough, and it slid through your fingers. I had to help you hold it firmly by pressing your fingers together and guiding your hand, and we eventually got it signed. The card was great!!

There is a nineteen-year-old close by, Craig. He broke his neck and will be paralyzed forever…Unless God intervenes. Be with him, Lord!

I feel so helpless at times, Craig, but our hope is in the Lord. One of the nurses shared her concerns about your despondency and said your friends need to come in and encourage you. After talking awhile, I dimmed the light on the way back into your room. I didn't want you to see I had been crying. Even though it was still early evening, I told you good night because we were both tired and needed rest. I couldn't even pray your verse with you tonight, Craig, because I knew I couldn't get through it without breaking down. I just reminded you Jesus was there and He was greater than anything. I kissed your hand good night and left. I took the underground tunnel to the parking garage, crying all the way, trying to remind myself God doesn't give us more than we can handle. In a way, my heart questioned Him, because I wasn't sure I could handle much more.

It was early evening so I just drove in Indianapolis; I'm not sure where I drove. I drove past an area on Emerson Street where a drive-by shooting had occurred, and I told the Lord I would volunteer for the next one, because I sure couldn't handle much more pain. I told the Lord He could just take me out – even with a rapist because going home to Heaven sounded good. There's no more pain and sorrow up there. That sounded so good!

Somehow, I ended up at Hardee's. I needed to eat and drink something so I could take my medicine for my bladder infection. I had been crying so much I didn't even want to go through the drive-thru. I parked close by and tried to collect myself. The smell of the grease nauseated me and I even wretched a couple times. I hadn't eaten all day, and my stomach hurt, but I wasn't sure I could force any food down. I decided on fries and a drink. I pulled through, got it, and parked in the lot to eat. My heart and soul were in such agony and distress – I can't express it – like groanings too deep for words (Romans 8:26) Craig, it was as if Jesus opened the passenger door, got in, and sat down beside me. He encouraged me by letting me know He was right there... that I could handle all He was allowing. He challenged me and said I either trusted Him or I didn't. When I told Him how bad my heart and soul hurt, He reminded me He knew! "Trust me, Linda," He challenged me. "We will take this one day at a time; I'll even show you what to do. Just show up every day, and we'll get through this together." Craig, this gave me a new perspective! Jesus has to do ALL the work; I just had to be there for you, and He would show me what to do. The mountain before us still seemed too big, but I had met the One who was responsible for getting us over it, if that was what He wanted.

I ate my supper and drove home to Bob and Ruth's. Dad had called there after checking at the hospital, and they told him I had left early. When I had told him I had spent two hours driving around crying, praying, and beseeching God, he was upset and scolded me. It was the appropriate ending to an absolutely horrible day. After telling Bob and Ruth good night, I went off to bed exhausted but couldn't sleep. Ruth came in. I told her about my unbearable heartache and the agony I felt, and I didn't know what to do. We cried together. She prayed with me and for me, and I finally went to sleep. (Bob and Ruth are our pastor's parents who happened to live in Indianapolis at the time of your wreck. They let me stay with them since week one).

Sunday, June 19 (Father's Day)

**Dad with Craig and brother Michael
on patio area at hospital – notice the casts.**

When I got to the hospital, you had already bathed. I shaved you. You smiled at me and reached your hand out to me. It was wonderful! My heart rejoiced!

Since you can't talk yet because of your trach, I wonder a lot about what you are thinking. Are you figuring things out yet? Do you understand the magnitude of everything? We read two chapters in the Bible and played a couple of Christian tapes. I just sat next to your bed and held your hand; we even took a nap. Dad and Mike came for Father's Day. We had practiced you picking up your gift in a sack and handing it to Dad. When you gave it to Dad rather awkwardly, he cried. Dad said it was his best Father's Day ever.

We watched videos together as a family. It was wonderful. A couple of Craig's rehab mates even joined us for the movies. Dad took his turn suctioning you. Craig, you passed some gas and just laughed (but no noise came out when you laughed). You still had your sense of humor.

We all go for a walk outside; of course you go in your rehab chair. We don't stay long, because your internal temperature control button in your brain isn't working well yet, and you don't tolerate the heat well. We don't have air conditioning at home, (I wonder if that will be a problem)!!

Michael is getting excited about I.W.U (Indiana Wesleyan University). This is Michael's last summer at home, and we are missing it.

Before Michael and Dad leave to go home, Michael has a one-on-one talk with you, Craig. Do you remember? After they leave, I get you ready for bed with our regular routine. You nod that you are sleepy. You nod you are not afraid. Your eyes are so big, as you search my face. We are tired. A new week of therapies awaits. I told you Jesus has angels at the corners of your bed. Jesus was there all the time, even when I couldn't be. I read your verse again tonight and remind you Jesus in you is greater than anyone or anything else.

I still catch myself saying things in the past tense about you, and it scares me. I wonder constantly IF God is going to restore you entirely. This is the desire of my heart (Psalm 37:4).

Monday, June 20

Craig, I woke up at 4:20 a.m., dreaming you called for help and were gagging. I called the hospital, and you were sleeping. The nurse had given you a sedative to help you sleep.

This morning, you had a swallowing test; you didn't pass. Some things were good but not good enough. The nurses said most don't pass the first time. The speech therapist plugged your trach, and you talked more. We have to start exercises to get your tongue, lips, and mouth ready for eating, talking, and swallowing.

You taught them gleaking: twisting your tongue and causing your salivary gland to squirt fluid. They are amazed how far it sprays.

You walked three steps forward and three steps backward on the parallel bars! Praise God!

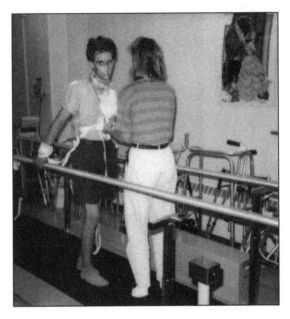

Craig's first three steps in Physical Therapy

You were so tired after your therapies! You worked hard! Ryan, your classmate, came to see you, and he gave you a haircut. He wanted to give you a buzz. I loved your beautiful hair so we settled on the trim. You smiled a lot. You knew he was there.

It's been one month, Craig! You try so hard at everything! Your bladder control and your awareness of needing to urinate is going well. You are dressing yourself some. You have come so far in one month, yet I can't imagine how far we have to go yet. You even had your first BM in the commode!! Go, Craig, go!

Tuesday, June 21

May 21 was the day of your wreck! June 21 was not a good day for you either. You are discouraged for some reason, and the nurses are trying to encourage you.

You and I have a long talk (only you can't talk). You listen and shake your head for me either "yes" or "no". I felt like the Lord helped me here. I asked you if you thought you were in a nursing home, you shook your head "no." I asked if you thought you were in a hospital, you shook your head "yes." I asked you if you had a wreck on your scooter bike, you shook your head "no." I asked if you were in a car wreck, and you shook "yes." I asked if you were afraid and you shook "yes". I proceeded to tell you where you were, at the trauma center in Indianapolis. I said you were going to be okay (I hoped) and that you would probably be able to talk again in a couple of weeks. The speech therapist was working on getting the trach out so you could talk with it plugged, and the mouth exercises were preparing you to eat again without the feeding tube. I explained that casts were on your legs not because your legs were broken but to keep your feet and ankles at proper angles, so you could walk later. I said that physical therapy was working on that.

I asked if you hurt anywhere, and you pointed to your head. I asked if it hurt now, and you shook "no." Your eyes look so big and bewildered, and I wonder how much you comprehend. I think I gave a pep talk about working hard in therapies, and God would do His part (whatever that would be).

We got several calls – Dad, Grandma, Aunt Sylvia, and your girlfriend's mom. I miss home so much; I wish this nightmare would end somehow.

Your therapists are just marveling at how well you are doing! You sat up well by yourself; you walked the full length between the parallel bars. Your speech therapist is amazed, too. I told her God was helping. She said "it was a good partnership" and "it sure was working."

Craig, progress seems slow from where I sit; we have so far to go, but they are all saying how far you have come already!

After supper, we practice writing your name with a crayon, your mouth exercises, and Bible reading. You are so tired that you forgot to tell me you had to urinate. You were nauseated and gaggy with your tube feeding.

You are really tired, so we get you ready for bed. I quote 1 John 4:4: "Greater is He that is in Craig that he that is in the world" and Psalm 91:11-12: "For He will give His angels charge concerning you, to guard you in all your ways, Craig." They will bear you up in their arms. I told you I loved you and I trusted Jesus. I kissed you goodnight and left you to His care with your tape playing our song, "The battle belongs to the Lord." Craig, you were asleep before I got out the door.

The halls are very quiet tonight because of the seriousness of the day's events. There is no laughter. I pray as I ponder all the families and pray for their pain. I keep thinking about Jamie. He's only 19 years old and paralyzed from the neck down, Lord. It was a diving accident while away at college; he went on a weekend canoe trip with his friends. His parents took him back to Chicago for rehab closer to home. Lord, please be with those parents and Jamie too. He went away to college and was carried home paralyzed! Lord, help those parents adjust to all that! There is tragedy and disappointment up and down the halls of a hospital. Be with each need, Lord!

I still have His hope. Craig will be healed, if it's God's will. God can heal paraplegics and quadriplegics too!! I wonder if Jamie knows Jesus. I pray for his parents and yet can't imagine their hurt, their shattered dreams. Craig, you are not paralyzed, so I can't understand. You are trapped in silence for now, and your mobility is only limited. "Lord, be there for them, and help them" is all I know to pray.

Wednesday, June 22

Your casts are off! Praise God!

You walked the entire length of parallel bars, rested, and did it again. You had lots of visitors. Aunt Sylvia and Uncle Ron came for a while.

I had to go home overnight, Craig, but I'll be back!!

Thursday, June 23

Craig, you wore shoes in PT.

You're in your new wheelchair.

You had a lot of company. You got a Christian T-shirt from your Sunday School class and a Michigan hat from your FCA director.

Craig, I can't believe all the people praying for you after five weeks.

You tried to sneak water out of the bathroom sink, but we caught you. Your swallow test is Monday! Please, Lord, help him pass it!

You had an episode with nausea, racing pulse, and blotching red skin. That wretching scares me with your feeding tube and trach. You took a nap. After resting, you felt better. You said you weren't afraid, so I left. I told you I loved you very, very much. You smiled and shook your head yes! Craig, I do! I still can't believe all this is happening. I hate to see you tied down. I worry you will gag and can't get up, but God is there, and I have to trust you to Him.

Friday, June 24

You rode a bike in PT today. You buckled belts and tied strings in O.T. and ate ice cream in speech. I practiced giving you water. You don't like the thickit they add to liquids to make them thick. Your water looks like clear applesauce or glue after it sets for a while.

Dustin, your friend on rehab, had a birthday party, and we went. Grandma, Grandpa, Aunt Claudia, and Cousin Wade went too. He loved opening all his gifts.

Jodi and Joey left today. She will be back in three weeks to get her artificial leg.

Pastor Bob and Susie came today to see you. They prayed with us before they left.

You were tired, so I left a little early. I reminded you of your angels and Jesus being there, as we prayed.

Saturday, June 25

Dad came and spent the day with us. After lunch we went to the patio outside. Jeff, Shane, Deanna, Mike, and Kenny were there. Craig, you mouthed that Jeff got a car; you had remembered from two weeks earlier! Praise God!! They had brought the movie <u>Ace Ventura: The Pet Detective</u> and a poster to put up. We watched the movie. Some more of your friends came; you got overstimulated and had one of your spells, so we had to clear the room for a while. After some rest and quietness, you were okay again.

Mr. LeMaster, your shop teacher, Pastor Dave, and Jill came. We all prayed with you.

Sunday, June 26

Dad stayed overnight and we got to your room by 10:30 a.m. You had been up and were back in bed. We let you rest and then toured some of the hospital with you. We took your picture in front of the trauma center.

We watched <u>Dancing With Wolves</u>. You had a lot of visitors again, including Uncle Ron and Aunt Sylvia. You had another episode of nausea and fast pulse, but this time, you also had a low-grade fever. You have a hoarse cough and maybe a sore throat, so you will get some antibiotics. After your visitors left, I left early too. You nodded you weren't afraid. W prayed, and I kissed you goodnight.

Craig, something neat happened. A neighbor lady, Ilene, who used to live down the road, called Dad over the weekend. Their family had moved out of the area to another state, but they had come back to visit, and she called Dad to tell him about a dream she had had: A young man was in bed but got up and walked. When she told her daughter about her dream and described the boy, her daughter told her it was you, and she told her mother about your wreck. The mother felt she needed to call us and tell us that you walked and were okay.

Laura, a classmate, also had a dream about you, and you were standing at your locker. She saw you on the track field dressed for track and you said "I'll be back".

Monday, June 27

Today is your swallow test. I got to the trauma center around 11:00 a.m. and you were in your wheelchair up by the nurse's station. They had downsized your trach; you kept trying to mouth and tell me something, but I couldn't understand. One of the nurses plugged your trach, and you said in your whispery voice that you were ready for the picnic I had promised. I promised you a picnic when and if you passed your swallowing test. You passed – liquids, here he comes!

You did well on your perception tests in O.T. You exercised four minutes on the step treadmill. Two of your therapists (O.T. and speech) taught me how to feed you; you are on a mechanical soft diet, so you had French fries and applesauce for your first meal. Later in the day, you ate a milkshake, some pears, and some wonderful regular, wet, cold, water (with <u>no</u> thickit).

You got another "silver bullet"– a suppository for a needed BM. Your tube feedings have made you constipated. You rested during your tube feeding. We did your foot and hand care; the dead thick skin around your nails sloughs off with ordinary activity, but with your limited activity, it accumulates around your nails. You always have such neat trimmed nails, so I get to give you a manicure and pedicure once in a while. All your calluses have disappeared.

You had a candy bar and some ice water today. We have to get 3000+ calories in you every day so you can get that feeding tube out. Your body will need that many calories daily for healing and rehab.

We prayed for the Browns!! (They lost their son in a tragic car wreck overseas).

Tuesday, June 28

We have to hold your liquids again. Your orange juice was in your trach secretions; you can still have solid food.

Your girlfriend came to see you again, and you gave her your stuffed baby seal (the one the hospital gave you). She got you a Myrtle Beach T-shirt. You looked real good in it.

A lot of friends visited! Praise God!!

Wednesday, June 29 (Roundtable Conference Day)

Your feeding group went well, even though we are using thickit again.

At your conference, all your therapists gave you rave reviews. You had exceeded all your goals. Things that were discussed will be our prayer concerns here and with your prayer warriors at home.

1) You have restricted cervical movement, and they aren't sure why.
2) You didn't do well on your perception tests (some areas profound, and some were severe). They reminded me that two weeks ago, you couldn't even be tested, and now you can be. These skills are some of the last to return, so relax, Mom, and don't worry yet.
3) You show physical weakness on your left side – your left leg, hand, and arm.
4) Your weak area in Speech was comprehension of long, complex paragraphs. You could write your spelling words, but you couldn't verbally say them. The verbal spelling takes one more brain function. Your reasoning skills were very low. You were not able to follow complex directions of three commands or more. My heart sank when they said you were at a seven-year-old level in some things. I choose to believe you aren't finished yet; we have only been at this three weeks. I know some weak spots, and we can practice some on our time.

It was a long, emotional day for Mom.

Thursday, June 30

Wow, Craig, you are walking with a roller walker and your gait belt. You walked from one room to another! Good job!

Your trach was plugged all of Speech, and you tolerated it well. In Speech, you are working on thinking – abstract thinking and reasoning. You struggle with things you cannot see. You had a hard time counting money in O.T. I love you so much, and it hurts to see your deficits, but you improve every day a little.

My visit with your social worker revealed their projection of your dismissal is September 13; that seems so far away. Michael will be away at college by then. The therapists are baffled at your progress and attribute it to a "higher power," who we know by the name of Jesus. I told her some of the things people had told us: their dreams, prayers, and peace, the stuff at school. She got goose bumps.

While coming to see you today, Craig, a car cut across all five lanes of I-65 heading north to Chicago. A couple of cars had to swerve to avoid an accident. I asked the Lord, looking heavenward, "Now, why didn't that guy wreck in all his stupidity and insanity?" God understands all those questions, thank heavens.

Friday, July 1

Your feeding tube is OUT!!! Praise God!!! Now we have to keep your diet at 3000+ calories a day. You get a lot of supplements, milk shakes, and snacks every day.

I questioned you about your neck: why you weren't looking left, etc. You said it was sore. I moved my chair to the left side of your bed to help you move and exercise your left side more.

Craig, you scared me to death today. We were changing your T-shirt, and I either caught your T-shirt under your trach cannula or you coughed, but something caused your trach to fly across the room. The nurses fixed it quickly, in spite of my panic.

Several of your friends came, and before they left, they formed a circle around you and prayed.

Saturday, July 2

I stopped on the way to the trauma center and got you a donut and some fruit. You enjoyed it. Count those calories!

You were complaining about numbness of your tongue, the left side of your face, some of the fingers on your left hand (particularly your left middle finger), your left rib area, and your left calf area. The nurse feels that these areas have probably been numb, and you are just now aware of it. Your on-call rehab doctor was in to check on you, and she was really impressed with your recovery; she sees you only when your rehab doctor is gone. You told her you hadn't said anything about the numbness earlier, because they couldn't do anything about it. She encouraged you to tell them anything and everything.

You have graduated to using the toilet in the bathroom instead of the bedside commode.

Sunday, July 3

I was late getting to the hospital this weekend; I think I am getting tired. As soon as I stepped off the elevator, there you were at the nurses' station and you said, "Where have you been?" It was wonderful to hear you complain.

One of the nurses had promised you a meatball sub for lunch, and boy, did you enjoy that!

We went for a walk off the unit today. Craig is starting to ask questions about the accident. I tell him what I know. He wants the ladies who sat with him in the field to come to Indianapolis and see him, if they can. He wants to thank them for praying for him and waiting with him until the rescue unit got there. He couldn't understand why the police didn't help him; he said, "Praying helped." I explained the police had to wait on the ambulance to move you, and the

Lord evidently sent the two mothers to wait with you, since I couldn't be there.

Flashback: Craig spent four days in a big room off from PICU while we were working out the arrangements with insurance. Craig was still in his coma. Later on, during Craig's rehab, after his trach was out and he could talk, Craig described this room and me standing by his bed. He remembers Michael and Dad sitting at the end of the bed watching the basketball playoffs on a big TV mounted on the ceiling. Craig tells me this weeks later, proving people can have lucid moments. What surprised me was his memory of it; his memory was supposed to be impaired! Praise God!

Craig also tells me the following story about seeing Jesus. He said Jesus was wearing a white robe and standing in a meadow with a deer close by and a rainbow in the sky; he said there was a tree nearby. He said Jesus' arm was stretched out, welcoming him to His Kingdom, and He called him by name. I asked Craig what He looked like and how he knew it was Jesus." Craig said like "the picture we have of Jesus, only His hair was shorter." Craig says Jesus gave him a choice. "Do you want to stay or go back?" Craig told Him, "Go back," and Jesus said, "So be it." Craig said he came back. He remembers a nurse telling him he had been in a bad wreck and that he had hurt his head. I asked him if he remembered anything else, and he said, "Yes, Mrs. Kelley was my second grade teacher."

Jesus with "long" hair.

Dad, Aunt Sylvia, and Uncle Ron are your visitors today.

Monday, July 4 (A holiday so no therapies)

Aunt Claudia, Cousin Wade, and Michael came to see you, while Dad and I went on a date. Everyone thinks I need a break. We went shopping, to a movie, and to eat at Outback Steakhouse.

We get a surprise tonight. The nurses are taking some of the rehab patients (in their wheelchairs) over to the parking garage to watch the fireworks over downtown Indianapolis. You had trouble tolerating the heat and humidity for that length of time; we gave you a lot of fluids and kept wiping the sweat off frequently. The fireworks were very good.

Tuesday, July 5

I went home to get my hair fixed. Dad stayed with you and went to therapies. Jim and Betty (from Florida) stopped to see you.

The staff is arranging for a neurologist to check your numbness. You have added all four little toes on your left foot to your list of numb areas!

While I was home, Craig, I got a call from another mom whose son had a head injury, and she answered a lot of questions for me. She lives close by, at Hagerstown; her son is Scott, and his accident was two and a half years ago; he started driving one year after his accident. We talked, and I cried, but her call really helped! Thank you, Lord!

Wednesday, July 6

Your neurologist came for a consultation. We talked a lot; he examined you, lightly sticking you with a safety pin to evaluate the numbness on different parts of your body. After an hour or so, he left to check your MRI and said he would be back. An intern was observing him, and he later returned to the unit to see Craig. He tells us the neurologist asked the radiologist for your MRI from several weeks ago. As the neurologist was looking it over closely, the radiologist asked him what he was looking for. The neurologist supposedly told him your symptoms – that you were numb on areas of your left side. The radiologist remarked that you were probably in a vegetative state. The neurologist then told him you weren't – you were talking and walking on the rehab unit. I think the intern just came up to look at you, Craig! Praise God!! I love you so much, Craig! The rehab people say we have to wait two years for healing and then see what your deficits are. God has taken care of each specific need, as we have asked! Praise God!!! The therapists are using heat and ultrasound on your neck to help with the stiffness and soreness.

Thursday, July 7

Evan and Erica leave today. We pray for them! You have your therapies and x-rays of your neck to see why your head doesn't sit straight on your shoulders!

Saturday, July 9

I got to the trauma center around 11:30 a.m. We went on a tour of the hospital just to get off the unit and practice our memory skills. We saw one of your doctors from PICU in the hall, and he talked to us to see how you were doing.

The FCA choir came and gave you a personal concert. You told them about seeing Jesus. They prayed for you. It was a blessing to me, too!

We walked with your Dad down to the lobby and cafeteria to check out the strawberry yogurt ice cream. Dr. Harvey from PICU recognized us and almost dropped his tray trying to get to you; you were sitting in your wheelchair. He seemed shocked, amazed, and almost speechless at your recovery. He had two other men with him, and he said a couple of medical things about you. He sat his food tray down, bent down closer, and asked you some questions (to see if you were really in there, I think). You told him about seeing Jesus, and he seemed amazed. We saw two of our nurses from PICU, and they marveled at your progress. These people didn't expect you to recover this quickly. I haven't decided yet but something special is going on!

Sunday, July 10

Dad came over to Indianapolis, so we went outside a couple of times and to the gift shop. We bought you a Fossil watch, so we can practice telling time.

Dad and I discuss the vehicle situation. When dad gets ready to go home, you thank him a second time for your watch.

Monday, July 11; Tuesday, July 12; Wednesday, July 13

Virginia came for a visit. We laughed, we talked, and we giggled. One afternoon we went to an outlet mall to shop.

Wednesday was conference day, and Dad came to this one. We asked for a day pass to take you away from the hospital for a day on the weekend. Your conference revealed "marked improvements" in all areas. They granted us a one-day pass to a local mall.

Tuesday, July 14

Today, you had a severe case of "mom-itis.". You are getting restless and bored with me as well as the hospital food and routine. I am tired of it all too. We supposedly have nine to eleven more weeks left.

My heart and mind are bombarded with a lot of questions, and they are not from the Lord. They make me doubt God's fairness, control, and love. Can we trust Him? I affirm to myself God loves us, and we cannot earn blessings or His protection, He gives those things according to His will and His way, to His children. We have to trust His love and the Word.

Craig has some questions too, as we do our devotions, and that's okay. God can handle them! Craig asked me why God didn't protect him when he was trying to "walk the walk" and follow Jesus. He talked about some of his class-mates who drink, drive, and have premarital sex; nothing happens to them. We talked about how God did protect him – maybe not the way I thought He would or should –and I reminded Craig that God sent those mothers to pray, kept his airway open, and put different people in needed places for us! God's ways aren't our ways, and we have to just keep telling ourselves God is in control and gets the final say. He's done a lot for us already. Craig listened!

I wrestled a long time with these questions. It hurts to see your child's brokenness – physically, emotionally, and in some ways spiritually as he sees people walk away or treat him differently. He questions his worth. I may be helpless or powerless to change people or things, but I am not hopeless as I petition our Father in heaven. I wonder silently what I or we did to deserve this, but that question is for Jesus. I feel like Satan is sifting Craig and us, but Jesus will pray for us that our "faith may not fail, and when we have returned, we can strengthen our brothers and sisters, because God is greater and will bring us through the flood waters." (Luke 22:31-32 and Isaiah 43:1-2).

I ponder, I pray, and we wait!

Friday, July 15

Craig, when you came back from therapies, you complained of blurred vision. They are getting you an appointment with a neuro-ophthalmologist! Wow (good spelling word)!

When I questioned you about your vision, you said you saw four of everything; then it was to two. Now, it is blurred vision up close.

Saturday, July 16

We took you out around 2:00 p.m., after a rest from morning therapies. We went to a big mall and got you a pair of blue jean shorts and a new T-shirt. We went to Olive Garden to eat. You were upset your girlfriend couldn't come, but it was wonderful having you out. Your wheelchair was hard at the restaurant, but it went well. We went to Bob and Ruth's. We had a prayer time.

It was a long afternoon for you. You complained that a finger and your left cheek are numb.

Sunday, July 17

Michael requested a dinner at Welliver's restaurant for his graduation. Aunt Sylvia and Uncle Ron will bring a pizza to you, and we go with the rest of the family to celebrate Michael's graduation. Even when I am away, my heart dwells on you and intercedes for your needs.

Michael has about six weeks of summer before college. Craig, we missed his last summer at home.

Monday, July 18

Craig, I wrestled all day with those questions that haunt us – the whys? Why me? I whined to the Lord all day about a lot of things! I miss Dad, Michael, and his last summer; I think I'm just tired of the hospital routine, food, etc.

The Lord had to shout at me to get my attention. "Sit down, Linda. Be quiet! And watch…" I did!!!

Saturday, July 23

Your physical therapist gave you your walking permit – no crutches, no walker, and no gait belt. You are safe to be up on your own. Praise God! We check you out. You go to a movie with Dad and your brother. We had a steak supper at Bob and Ruth's with corn on the cob, green beans, cucumbers, rolls, and the works! Thanks Bob and Ruth! It was delicious!

Sunday, July 24

I signed you out, and we drove home to church. Everyone was shocked to see you when you walked in!! It was truly wonderful to be at home, to be together in church.

We had a big family chicken dinner from Famous Recipe and homemade ice cream.

Dear old mom made you rest after lunch, because your brain needed to rest. You got to see your room. You couldn't remember what your room looked like.

Several of your friends came by around 3:00 p.m. You watched a movie on the VCR.

We left around 6:00 p.m. to go past a couple places to see people, and we arrived back at the trauma center at 8:30 p.m.

You did well. You tolerated no air conditioning which was one of my concerns. You tolerated a long day of stimulation, and it was absolutely wonderful being home, even if only for a few hours.

Monday, July 25

One of your main primary care nurses is transferring off the unit. We had a long talk, while you were at your therapies. She doubts you will fulfill your lifelong dream. She feels the technology and advancement in medicine over the years is the reason for your comeback, yet she is even amazed at your return. I watch, I listen, and I ponder what the Lord is doing.

Dad called. He misses me and Craig! Mike does too! Isn't it nice to be missed?

Wednesday, July 27

Your eye appointment with your neuro-ophthalmologist revealed two problems.

1) Your eyes don't go inward to help focus.
2) Your blurred vision is within a limited 8-14 inches. The little switch in the brain that tells your eyes to switch from near vision to far vision is damaged and hopefully will correct itself in time. Again, two years of healing and then accept whatever deficients are left.

You rode a skateboard (to improve your balance) on the patio, fell, and skinned your knees/hand. Your therapist almost had a heart attack, but you love PT. Your balance is improving!!

Sunday, July 31

We came home again and went to church. Just to see Craig walk on his own again makes my heart rejoice. I went to the altar to thank God for all He had done. Craig came and joined me at the altar; he asked for his heart's desire – to be independent from mom and go back to school. God knows and understands it all! People don't realize that God had to completely rewire his brain. Craig is even better than before.

Lord, please show them-confirm it on the C.A.T. (California Achievement Tests). Show Craig you have too!

Craig later told me that as he was sitting there, he did not want to go to the altar. I had told Craig I was going just to tell the Lord thank you for all He had done and to ask His will in several matters heavy on our hearts: the school issue, the upcoming C.A.T. tests, and a couple of other things. Craig reached over, poked me, and said he was going too. The Lord had nudged him to go! Craig went! Praise God! Craig heard His voice and then obeyed it!!

Monday, August 1

Craig was released to go home overnight on the weekends until discharge. Those days home get us prepared by helping us adapt or adjust to the home settings while still anchored to the therapists.

All the steps at home had been an issue with his balance off, but that issue resolved with improvement of his balance. Craig even got rid of that gait belt which he had been wearing under his shirt as a safety measure for us to catch him and keep him from losing his balance.

Friday, August 5

Craig gained his independence at the hospital. He takes himself to and from therapies in different areas of the hospital. (This privilege tests memory skills and it shows responsibility. He has to watch the time and remember appropriate articles to take. My heart rejoices to see you be responsible. Your memory is better than mine.

Tuesday, August 9

We will spend the next two days across town doing your testing (C.A.T. tests) at your neuropsychologist's office. They are checking your I.Q. and for any holes (deficients) in your learning process. This will help determine your school capabilities and needs, placement, etc.

This day was truly a challenge. We arrived in plenty of time to get you across town, but your paperwork to leave the hospital to go across town hadn't been completed, and that person who needed to sign it was not available. The insurance company and the doctor's office couldn't resolve the issue of coverage for the testing. We finally got everything resolved, arrived on time, and reported in with the receptionist who forgot to tell them we have arrived. We started over 30 minutes late in testing!! Craig and I had prayed together for this; he was worried, nervous, and hates testing!

The Lord challenged me to fast and pray for this. I really felt a spiritual battle going on here. I read, prayed, and really interceded for the testing, naming the specific areas I knew they would be doing. The testing was broken down into two three-hour sessions in the morning (since mornings are best for head injury patients – they are fresh physically and mentally from the night's rest). I got tired of the waiting room chairs and darkness, so I took a walk, continuing to pray. The receptionist kept me posted. I could leave and come back at lunchtime to get Craig. I sat in the car and prayed; it was an absolutely beautiful day and my heart was anxious for Craig, this testing would reveal his mental faculties or the lack thereof. The Holy Spirit would prompt me to pray about a specific need, and I'd speak it to the Lord!! I practiced the principles of covering Craig and his brain with the resurrected power and authority of Jesus. His blood covered Him, and His name was used to seal the promise of who Craig was/is in Christ! This will only make sense to born-again

Christians, but we have certain privileges afforded to us (as Christians) if we choose to use them. I didn't want doubt and fear to plague Craig's mind; fatigue was an enemy to Craig, so I prayed against it.

When I returned to get you for lunch, you were doing so well that they wanted to continue after lunch. You didn't seem fatigued, so I took you to a fast food place for lunch and then back for more testing.

On Wednesday, we returned for the rest of your testing. Again, the areas they were testing you in went so well that they continued after your lunch break. You didn't seem fatigued at all. God continued to show me how to pray for you and stand in the gap as your intercessor. Those last couple of hours, I sensed you were getting tired, but you hung in there. Craig, it was an awesome responsibility and privilege God gave me, but He showed us He was in it all! We asked Jesus to autograph your results, so all involved would know it was of God Almighty.

Your testing later revealed a normal IQ of 95. When I read over it, it was sort of Greek to me, but the final evaluation was you could return to school full-time in the fall with only a math modification, and hopefully arrange your classes, so the morning hours when you are less tired would be your harder classes. You were to be plugged into the L.D. program to assist you and monitor your weak areas. We decided to cut class load from six to five classes. You would require more time, at first, for completing tests and assignments.

This was a lot different than originally predicted. The therapists and your neuropsychological doctor had indicated you would be wheelchair-bound your first semester or so due to the fatigue factor, and home-bound teaching the first semester might be the best solution for returning to school. This changed after they saw your exceptional progress. The hospital arranged a meeting for the school's guidance coun-selor and L.D. teacher to come to the hospital for a roundtable to discuss your needs, your areas of present weakness, and to assist in developing an educational plan (I.E.P.).

These last few weeks of therapy at the hospital were full of preparing Craig for his release home.

Craig had a tendency to drag his one toe (left I think) when he got tired – at end of the day - so physical therapy was videotaping his walk and gait to fit him with a brace. Craig questioned me one day after therapy about what was going on, and I explained the problem and the solution was a shoe brace. Craig was not too happy and said no brace. He told me I needed to pray about this <u>some more</u>; I told Craig I had, and he could go to the Father and ask for himself. Craig prayed about this. Over the next few physical therapies, his therapist (who is also a Christian) saw such improvement he did not need a brace on discharge and was released from PT before he was even discharged from OT or Speech. Reflecting back, Craig had come so far in three months – from his coma to not being able to sit, move a finger, or hold his head up. The first few times on the treadmill after he graduated from the parallel bars, Craig couldn't conceive right from left, so we had placed stickers on his hips – an owl and a cat. When we were trying to help him tell his brain to lift his left leg and hip-take a step-right leg and hip take a step-we used the owl and cat: owl, cat, owl, cat, to teach him how to walk. When he progressed well enough to walk correctly, I remember him trying to run and his therapist running beside him with a gait belt and how with his balance off he'd run into the walls. He walked on a 2x4 to correct his balance or a controlled skateboard exercise. It was marvelous to see how far he had come, to realize all we take for granted outside a rehab center, and how blessed we were at Craig's recovery.

Speech is where Craig's greatest deficiencies were. Craig started doing two Speech sessions in the morning and two in the afternoons. I praise God for the support and assistance Craig got as he did these extra therapies. He got extra computer time or homework for areas we could work on in evenings. Craig worried and asked about his deficits, but I reminded him if we do our part, God is responsible for the rest, and that's all we can do. I jokingly told him I didn't have a brain injury, and I couldn't figure out some of their brain teasers (or perception tests) in O.T.

I later learned that after I left in the evening or after breakfast in the mornings before therapies, Craig would go down to the mats in the corner of the kitchen area and do set ups, push ups, and other exercises to build his strength. Craig was fighting the good fight, completing their course at the hospital above and beyond their requirement – for whatever God had for him in the future. Philippians 3:12-14 says , "Not that I have already obtained it, or have already become perfect, but I press on in order that I may lay hold of that for which also I was laid hold of by Christ Jesus. I do not regard myself as having laid hold of it yet; but one thing I do: forgetting what lies behind and reaching forward to what lie ahead, I press on toward the goal for the prize of the upward call of God in Christ Jesus."

Jesus was/is the author and perfecter of our faith, so He was going to have to get Craig through this and lead him where He wanted him. I just came along with Craig. God had given me a front row seat in a miracle, and it was so hard watching all of it, but again, 1 Corinth 10:13 is true, it's up to us whether we believe and practice it! The choice is ours. The saying, "I don't know what the future holds, but I know WHO holds the future" was really true in our lives. If God wanted Craig's brain rewired and fully restored, He would be the one to do it, and only He could lead us into that future and fulfill whatever destiny Craig was to live.

D Day (Discharge Day)

August 12 was that day we had longed for and Craig had worked so hard for. Remember our original projected release was around September 16 or so. After morning therapies and saying goodbye, we ate lunch on the unit; Craig received his rehab graduation certificate. Craig had asked to see the MRI that gave his grim prognosis, and it had been sent to the rehab floor. Craig was standing in front of the x-ray light box when his neurosurgeon walked by. He told Craig everything white was not good, and that the person's brain viewed on the x-ray box should not be standing in front of it. Craig had several large areas of bruising, and several white dots showing the shears they mentioned, and again my heart rejoiced at what God had/was doing. He visited the helicopter pad, sat in the helicopter that had transported him, and met some of the people.

We said our goodbyes with some hesitancy – maybe more so for me. Craig couldn't wait to get home. I had listened 'well' while I was there and wondered what awaited us. As a mother, I had been forewarned; rehab was the easy part, and going home would turn out to be the worst part, but a necessary part on the road of recovery. I couldn't understand what could/would be worse than rehab...the easy part, yet I couldn't imagine what could be harder than waiting to see if your child would live or die, and if he lived, would he be okay? What context did okay mean? What could be harder than helping your child 'pick up the pieces' to his life; help him learn how to walk, talk, shave, tie his shoes, write his name – what could be harder than that? My heart had ached every day and also rejoiced at each and every task Craig had relearned. Craig had worked so hard when the mountain seemed so steep, yet he did it – one step at a time, one day at a time, with those around us cheering him on.

They (the staff) reiterated we would never be the same, we wouldn't look at life or any situations the same. We were different people now. How my heart longed to come home and everything would be okay! Little did I know.......

Craig slept most of the way home. My heart was filled with thanksgiving and anticipation during that one and a half hour ride home. Craig had come so far, but we still had fifteen months to travel before we would know the end results...or extent of his accident and his deficients.

My heart rejoiced when I pulled in the drive. <u>We</u> had made it <u>home</u>. I felt, maybe wanted, life to get back to normal, if there is such a thing as normal. To sleep in our beds, enjoy our "little corner of the world-our backyard," home cooking, to be around our family and friends, and especially to see and be with Dad and Mike again would be wonderful. Mike had about three weeks before he was off to college. There was so much to do too!!

Craig's friend Theo was there to welcome him with a giant poster and balloons. Our pastor's wife and Kirstin were there too!! Some of the ones I thought would be there to welcome us weren't, and that hurt. It didn't matter!! We were home!!! If only people knew how hard Craig had worked to get here today, my heart sighed, and we unpacked all of his clothes, gifts, and souvenirs from our three months away.

Craig had nine days till school started. We made our first contacts for outpatient Speech and O.T.

Life was very busy those next few weeks. My journaling stopped. The rest of the story is completed more as events happened instead of daily and weekly reports of progress.

The Nightmare Begins......

They had encouraged us to get counseling to get through the memories and the grieving process. We arranged for Craig to be plugged into our youth pastor's schedule for counseling and talking and adjusting to his "new" perspective of life. I was so naïve; I guess I thought life eventually would be "normal" again – whatever normal is. When you are in the rehab setting, they become your support, your cheerleaders, your encouragers, your listeners. At home, you realize you are on your own; their support is a phone call or pager away, but the stress and pressure is ever-present. I even felt that Paul didn't always understand my concern in many issues, because he hadn't been there and seen all the stuff I had seen.

That's probably one thing I missed the most. There was never a time the therapists told Craig you can't do that – they gave him a task to do and then watched to see if he had the skills to do it. If he didn't, they backed up and taught him, helped him to accomplish the task that lead to the next step, always positively encouraging him to keep trying, try a little harder, just give a little more till he built his strength and endurance to the point of his discharge.

The school issue... School and all of its facets became Craig's biggest challenge. If I had to do this part over, I would probably change the way we handled his return to school. The old cliché is true – hindsight is better than fore-sight and the best of intentions.

When the school needs were addressed, the wise ones recommended his core subjects be in the morning, since that's when he would be sharpest (after a night's rest), with after-noon maybe a study hall and vocational class. They suggested a typing class to work on motor skills, hand/eye coordi-nation, and of course L.D. support. We switched his math class from a higher math to more of a review general math and recommended a math tutor. We couldn't find a teacher willing to tutor, so we trusted Craig to God again to work out the details. I couldn't change a schedule and God didn't either, so Craig had to do the adjusting – surviving might be a better word here. Study hall was first thing, and English was last period of the day. Craig, I later learned, slept a lot here, but he completed his assignments, survived his teacher, and got his credit. To my astonishment, I never heard much from his teachers. I trusted his L.D. teacher and relied on her to stay on top of things for me, as I distanced myself from the issue. We told Craig he had to do the adjusting-whatever he needed to do to get his credits. I got a second set of books from the guidance counselor. I read the history and literature stuff and quizzed Craig verbally at home. Craig had some deficits in the early part of recovery with inductive/deduc-tive reasoning skills, test questions, etc, and this is where his L.D. teacher saved his life. There were a couple of teachers who wouldn't attend the preschool information meeting about Craig's needs in these areas. Again, I had to count on his L.D. teacher to check on these classes. Craig's typing teacher chose not to attend the meeting. When Craig asked a simple question about how to set margins, he was given this answer: "you learned that in 7th grade." Craig did, but his memory bank had been deleted, and he needed reminders. If it wasn't for his friend Theo, Craig wouldn't have survived typing class. Craig was hurt when he was humiliated in front of his peers by his teacher. This showed Craig the teacher didn't value him enough to teach (or reteach) something simple. This is where Craig's self esteem plummeted, and I was totally helpless. Craig couldn't remember where the restrooms were, his locker combinations, etc. Then add the gawks and stares of the kids and some of the teachers' insensitivities. They responded to Craig differently, treated him differently. A few kids even mocked him and his God, asking Craig where his God was the night he needed Him. One kid got in his face and asked if he was in there. Craig couldn't hit back, yet when he got home, he shared his hurts and his disappointments in teachers, friends, and peers. These people hadn't changed a bit probably. Craig was the vulnerable one, and things were overwhelming. Craig was told he would look at life differently, and he did. Where Craig had been supported and encouraged to overcome in his rehab setting, he had only two or three who were encouraging him (and Mom didn't count). The fatigue factor didn't help. This is where I should have just shortened his day, but Craig had worked so hard to get back to school. The therapist encouraged him to try it. Mom seemed to be the odd one out in our discussions. Yet I felt the very people Craig wanted to be around were making him doubt his worth. The sin of omission is probably the most hurtful one – people stared at him with pity but never acknowledged him. He wanted to be treated the same as he was before. He covered a lot of his hurt with humor and jokes, yet he hurt so bad inside.

Craig also had an unquenchable desire to learn the details of his accident. He started on the emotional journey of "putting together all the pieces". He revisited the accident scene. We had pictures of the truck and my journal. He wanted to visit the trauma Emergency Room and meet the doctor who had taken care of him. Before we left the rehab hospital, he visited the roof where he landed. Also, he met the pilot and person who had been with him on his flight; he even sat in the chopper. I had tried to talk with the local E.R. physician to no avail, but our guidance counselor arranged a meeting one day. The guidance counselor took him to visit the Emergency Room and he met his physician. He was amazed at Craig's progress.

I can't put into words all the emotions and frustrations I felt as a mother at the mercy of a cruel and heartless world around Craig, but I prayed, I cried, and I trusted God again, because I was helpless, but God was all-powerful. Only He could help Craig dig his anchor deep in Him.

Craig started losing his beautiful hair about two to three weeks into school. He would find a handful in the tub after his shower. He'd run his hand through his hair at school, and it would come out like a shedding cat's. He wasn't going bald though. We visited our local doctor who assured us this was common after such a traumatic event and that Craig would be okay. To spare Craig any further embarrassment at school, he took his friends up on a "buzz" – the new trend of the junior class. Craig talked his friend into buzzing his hair in one of his classmates' garages. That took care of that problem, only most of his friends didn't realize the reason he did it. When I saw him, I almost cried – but I understood and admired his courage to solve his problem.

Craig was a member of the Fellowship of Christian Athletes (FCA) at school. They chose to let Craig share his testimony at their concerts throughout the area. They sang songs that said, "God is in Control, Be Strong and Courageous," etc. Craig and others told the story of Craig's accident: his injuries, his recovery, God's promises, and the miracles God did (for Craig and us).

All of the things going on at school with his classes, his friends, the withdrawal of friends, Craig's personal journey through the grieving process and putting all the missing pieces together got overwhelming at times. We had been warned all this would happen! Being naïve, I felt we could get through this; after all, we made it through rehab. I even thought maybe Craig was imagining people's lack of acceptance, but after talking to Theo and a couple other friends, Craig wasn't too far off. I had busied myself with work and outpatient therapy appointments after school, helping with homework, etc. I didn't have time for renewing my friendships, but Paul had noticed people treated us differently too; he mentioned it to me. When I sought wisdom from the pros on our return visit to Indianapolis, they assured me everything happening was typical. This all was the stuff they said makes going home so difficult. Reality is such a shock. You expect support and get silence or rejection. Everyone expected the old Craig to show up. When he didn't, they treated him as a reject, and refused to accept him. His humor regarding the accident made everyone feel awkward, which only isolated him more. Most kids, unless they have had to deal with real life issues like Craig had, don't have time or the compassion and understanding needed. We were told most wouldn't wait the two years Craig's brain and body needed to heal to give Craig a chance to return to his "best" possible self. Adolescents don't have time to wait – they live life fast and furious, full of activities, and Craig didn't fit into that pattern.

Those Tough Questions

Craig was asking some heavy questions now – which was normal. *Why me?? God, I was a good guy, so why didn't you protect me? Where were you when I needed you?* Again, Craig asked some of the same questions I had asked.

After he got his voice back, we would do devotions. The biblical truths we read helped Craig search for answers to those questions. Craig had to travel this road alone. My answers weren't always what he wanted to hear or what I wanted to hear. God does let bad things happen to good people. Joseph and Job are two examples. We went over their stories. Their lives had misfortune, but God was still there. Their part was to remain faithful.

Craig had to work this out between himself and His creator. We encouraged him as well as his neuropsychologist to read the book <u>When God Doesn't Make Sense</u>. His neuropsychologist had recommended <u>When Bad Things Happen to Good People</u>, but we chose the Christian alternative, and Craig read it. He struggled emotionally and psychologically. He wondered if he would have been better off staying in Heaven, when Jesus gave him the option. We stood our ground spiritually for Craig, denouncing the things, people, and ways the enemy was using to rob Craig of all his joy of what God had done in his life (John 10:10).

Craig was doing well in school, and his therapies were concluded by December 1994. It had been projected he would need therapies for months, even beyond that first year (due to the extent of his injuries). By Christmas, Craig's reading skills were up to grade level, his memory skills had improved more, and he was released from all therapies. No more outpatient therapies after school! Craig was so pleased. What a praise and another sign of God's hand in his recovery!

Craig was still very frustrated and unhappy. His anger and frustration got worse and worse. We made a trip to the hospital to talk with those who understood and could give some impartial insight. The social worker talked to me after talking to Craig, and she shared some of Craig's general concerns and said TBI kids do better in a new environment with people who never knew them before. She indicated adolescent kids don't have time to wait. Too much is going on in their lives in a lot of areas, and they don't have time to wait on Craig; they expected the old Craig to reappear, and when he didn't, they didn't let him back into their circle. I remember asking, "Are you telling me we need to sell our house and move because of people's ignorance and unacceptance?" She very seriously said, "Yes, sometimes that's best." I was shocked, dumbfounded, and hurt. Needless to say, we didn't sell our house. We coped; we dealt with the problems as they arose. We reinforced to Craig that we can't change people or their reactions to us. We must be the ones to press on, to exhibit grace and unconditional love. That's all we can do. We have to let God heal our emotional hurts from the inside out.

I was intrigued how the enemy of Craig's soul could torment him so and make him doubt his life was worth anything; a few times he wished he had stayed in Heaven. A lot of questions were robbing Craig of his joy and peace. How could he find that peace?

Christmas Break 1994 was a brief oasis for me where I had a day or two to catch my breath and sit and rest. His outpatient therapies were done! I remember sitting in a chair one day and just staring into the quietness of our house. I couldn't believe we were all home together. Mike was home from college, and I was off work from the school system. (I worked with EH kids in another local school system). I was so tired and weary, but glad we made it to Christmas Break. I cried and my heart rejoiced, yet it was burdened for the future. For the moment, I sat, rejoiced, and just wept!!

There was a particular incident we must not fail to mention. One time Craig ran away. It was prior to an FCA concert. Craig was at one of the FCA functions one Sunday evening. Something was said by someone, and Craig left the church. When we got there, we were told Craig had left in the car, but no one knew where he went. Paul went looking at a few places and then went home. I returned to the concert, because that is where Craig thought we would be. This was the night that another mother was going to share about the emotional hurts of life. As I heard her talk, I understood why it was good Craig was not there and why he had left. Even though hurts had driven him away, God used it for good. At the end of the concert, Paul called me to let me know he had gotten a call from the rehab hospital 70 miles away. Craig had driven back to see the nurses on the rehab unit. When we arrived, Craig was sitting at the nurses' station, and he was even out of place there. He had parked his car in the parking garage, and he got a flat tire. He had planned to see them and then go on to Chicago, where no one would know him. I praised God for that flat tire; I praised God for keeping him safe, sparing him from more hurt at the concert, and I praised God for being sovereign. I praised God for going before to prepare, protect, and spare us from things unseen to our human eyes and hearts.

Paul changed the tire, and we headed home with Paul driving the car Craig had driven over there, and Craig riding with him. I followed them back home just praying and pleading the blood of Jesus over them, the car, Craig's mind, etc. The Lord impressed upon me that Craig needed to go before the Lord and give Him his anger and disappointments. Even if he couldn't honestly say he knew how to give it to God, Craig needed to ask God to help him let go of the hurt and the anger. God released Craig as soon as he prayed. Craig asked for help, and he spoke names and things that had hurt him. Craig felt so light and free. We were up till 1:00 or 2:00 a.m. before we got all of it settled with God. Craig was up to go to school to tell his friends what God had done. Craig was able to praise God for being able to walk, for being alive. He was free, praising <u>God</u>, laughing, so happy!

Craig did survive his junior year and got all 10 credits with B's and C's. We had made it a year with one year to go. He even went to his junior prom with a friend and had some good memories. The spring and summer of his junior year were monsters! Craig needed his wisdom teeth out, so we did that in two trips to the oral surgeons over that spring break of 1995.

The last day of school in June 1995 was the first day of my new job. We needed more money for Michael's college tuition. We also used his summer vacation to get that ugly trach scar reconstructed; at the same time Craig needed more surgery for another medical problem (not related to his accident). The two local surgeons worked together and took turns in surgery to get both done at the same time, which was wonderful for Craig. Both surgeries went well. Recovery time was minimal and uneventful! Thank heavens!

Summer arrived and Craig got a job with the local parks department. He worked at the area baseball diamonds, selling concessions and getting supplies to all the diamonds. We had him tested on a referral from his rehab doctor to determine his driving ability. She said he was ready; I remember her telling him he was one of three of her rehab patients who had recovered 100 percent. She marveled at that and told him he could go to King's Island (he had asked about that for his school trip). We gave all the glory to God for his recovery.

Regarding that driving test and concerns you must be having, there was a whole battery of tests trained specialists put Craig through to make sure he was physically, mentally, and psychologically ready to drive. He had written tests (over laws, etc), a test on a driving simulator, and an actual driving test in Indianapolis during lunchtime rush hour at a busy intersection in that big city. The two driving testers intentionally tried to get him upset and distracted, and he did wonderful, passing with flying colors.

This was a big issue between me and the Lord regarding trust and him driving again. Part of me wanted to keep him from driving again, so he'd never wreck, but we saw a lot of kids seriously injured while being a passenger. I came home happy for Craig, but a little upset with the Lord, because I wasn't ready for this. I remember sending Craig to get some stamps at the local post office and flour at the small town grocery store about ten miles from our home. It was daytime and I was an emotional mess the whole time he was gone, crying yet praying for him. Craig asked why couldn't I trust him if those specialists said he was okay. We had let him drive some with us after his clearance from the driving academy, but we loved him and didn't want him to have to go through that pain again. It took me a while to not pace the floor and worry. The first time he drove at night was a biggy too. If he was a few minutes late getting home from work, I'd start to worry. God and I <u>talked</u> a lot about <u>Trust</u>!

Craig's senior picture.

His senior year arrived! We had his senior pictures made during the late summer; we were ready to get high school over with, and we made some changes for a successful/positive senior year. We placed Craig in a work-study program, where he went to school part of the day and then worked the rest of the day. This limited his time in the school environment and gave him a chance to be in a workplace. It was the best decision we ever made. He worked from September to December at the local sheriff's department. Craig wanted to pursue law enforcement. His job raised his self-esteem and confidence, and he did great. He loved his job. Praise God!

But even his senior year had a flaw. During Labor Day weekend, he had a lawn mower accident while mowing a friend's yard for extra money. It was the Saturday before Labor Day; I was at work (in a local physician's office) when I was called and told what had happened. I will never forget that day! When I got to the same local emergency room where he had been airlifted out of 16 months before, I can't describe the feeling I had. I walked in there and saw him lying on a stretcher with an IV. A nurse was working on his hand, and I saw his three fingertips lying in an ice bucket. I looked at Craig, excused myself, and went out to collect myself. Craig's youth pastor/counselor greeted me on my exit from the Emergency Room. I was so angry at God, and I told him so. "This isn't fair." I made a fist and hit the wall. My heart felt as if it would explode in my chest from the heartache. Craig said something too; I will never repeat it, but it pierced my soul. His senior year was starting with another tragedy, more surgery, and a lot of doctor appointments. The local emergency room doctor sent us to a surgery center specializing in hands. We arrived on Saturday afternoon, and Craig spent that day in surgery. The doctor used an arm block for the surgery, so we could take him home later that night. This was a long, long, long day for Paul and me. We sat there in unbelief. How could all this be happening again? The place was almost deserted because of the holiday. We prayed off and on. Only one other lady was there by herself, crying at times. We talked to her and found out that her husband had fallen and cut the heels of his feet with a lawnmower; we cried and prayed with her. Her husband had surgery and was waiting to be admitted. Our pastor's father came to see us in the Emergency Room area!! I remember telling him, "I don't understand," and we had had enough, and Craig had had enough.

Surgery went well. They wrapped Craig's hand like a huge ball. You could see only his thumb sticking out at the side. We got home late that Saturday night. Craig was zapped with all the pain medicine. Paul and I drove home in silence. I remember having to keep his hand elevated all night. I didn't sleep well.

That Sunday, we were so tired, so we slept in, and none of us went to church. Two of our pastors visited after church.

They weren't sure what to say but reminded us that God did love us and would be there for us. Paul did not say much that day. In my heart, I told God that He would have to show me the good in this, because I just couldn't imagine what it would be (Romans 8:28)! I cannot put the devastation of my soul into words here. I put my Bible on the shelf and decided to take a break from religion until God showed me!

We made several trips back and forth to the hand center. His little finger had multiple fractures. A "giant-looking hat pin" stuck out the end of his little finger holding all the pieces in place. The nail bed and fingernail had been damaged and repaired; we had to change the dressing on this finger every night after the discarding of the original surgery dressing. His index finger lost the pad, and a new one had to be grafted off the palm of his hand. His index finger had been sewed to his palm, after a small window had been made into the palm of his hand.

He had two other surgeries plus a couple more simple surgeries to remove the nail bed fragments from the other two fingers which lost their distal ends. One school night, during the dressing change, that "hat pin" came out about an inch, while I was removing the old dressing. I sat there in shock. What do we do now? We contacted the surgeon on call, and she told us to come over. We were 1¾ hours from the hospital, but we loaded up and went. That late at night, there isn't as much traffic on the highways. We got there around midnight; the surgeon on call was great to Craig. She x-rayed his hand, said it was healed, and gently removed the pin. Craig saw his finger under the x-ray machine and how it had healed. He was amazed. We got home around 2:00 a.m.

The graft of his index finger did so well they took pictures of it. They said the nail bed would probably never be flat or grow out smoothly. It healed beautifully, and he has a normal fingernail today! God was showing Himself to us in several little ways; they spoke to my heart. I had to smile at God and say, "Okay! I'm watching!" The surgeon even said Craig's index finger was good enough for pulling a trigger, if he still wanted to be a police officer (that door was still open).

God had allowed Craig to share his story about his wreck, seeing Jesus, and his dreams with his hand surgeon. I remember sitting there in that side chair, as Craig and the surgeon talked. This man was very educated and rich. Craig asked if he had gold cufflinks and a gold watch on. Craig just talked about Jesus and all He had done in his recovery, and his hand. That surgeon put down his pen and chart and just listened to every word about Jesus. I got tears in my eyes and told God He had won! He had shown me a lot of good out of all of this. I jokingly told God if he needed another doctor to hear about Jesus, all He had to do was give me their name and address, and I would write a letter to him; please do not arrange a one-on-one encounter through a tragedy. Craig asked me on the way home if I thought that doctor believed him. I assured Craig the doctor had listened to every word he had said. The part about seeing Jesus really got his attention; that was when he stopped looking at his finger and just sat and listened.

Craig worried that people would think his hand was ugly, and no girl would ever want to hold it. "Okay, Lord." I said, "send someone to hold his hand." Craig would carry that hand in his pants pocket most of the time, hiding it. Then God sent a girl to show Craig it was not "grotesque." She was a Christian girl at an ice skating rink. Craig was trying to keep his hand hidden. Finally, she insisted Craig trade hands while they were skating, and she told him it wasn't that bad. I'd like to think God knew Craig's insecurity. He sent that special girl at that certain time to show Craig his hand was okay.

The FCA (Fellowship of Christian Athletes) had their concert one night at the school cafeteria. We went, and Craig used that hand openly, so I knew God was working there. One morning in church, the congregation was singing praise songs, and as I looked forward towards Craig, he lifted his injured hand in praise to God. It was opened up for God to see, and my heart rejoiced again; my heart was praising again. If Craig could praise God, I needed to also. I asked Craig if good had come from all this. I wanted to hear his perspective. He shared that his left hand and arm had been weaker from his wreck. With his right hand wrapped and out of use for several weeks, he had to use his left hand more. Consequently, it had gotten stronger, and he had more strength and fine motor and agility with it now. He remembered sharing Jesus with the hand surgeons and therapists at the hand surgery center and said God wanted us to be His witnesses anywhere and everywhere at any time.

Back to school stuff: the people at Craig's jobs worked with his hand situation. Everyone was great and supportive. With budget issues at the jail, Craig worked the second semester at a grocery store. He enjoyed it too, and it went well with the responsibility, people skills, and his positive evaluations edifying him, and it built his self-confidence, self-esteem, and self-image.

His senior year was over. Graduation night was emotional for us. We were so glad he had made it and could move on. Paul and I got a tiny glimpse of how his classmates treated him; only two or three actually said goodbye to him personally. Craig stood and watched his former friends take group pictures, and he wasn't included. Our close family never came over to the reception either, and that meant those wishing Craig congratulations were very few. Our youth pastor came, and one Christian couple who had been prayer warrior friends drove 1½ hours to see Craig graduate; they came over to say hi, but I knew Craig's heart ached. This chapter of Craig's life (school) was over, and I was so relieved, so glad to move on.

Somewhere between his junior year and graduation, we were asked to share Craig's journey at the Brain Institute;

Craig and I sat on a panel for parents to ask questions after giving a brief story of what had happened during Craig's traumatic brain injury (TBI). Paul and I were on a parent committee and served as a mentor to another couple whose daughter had had a TBI, so God was using us to help others.

After Graduation

Two weeks after graduation, Craig moved to a town about forty-five minutes away. He had been discouraged by many from pursuing a career in law enforcement. He loved his occupational therapy assistant's job description there in rehab, so he decided to try it. He enrolled in a community college in that town and actually got free board for staying with a quadriplegic who needed someone for a.m. assistance (to get ready for work) and p.m. assistance (to get ready for bed). Craig didn't know a soul there. It was hard for Craig to go, but he went due to our encouragement and the fact that this was the only door God allowed to open.

He got in some college prep classes and traveled at his own pace. He did very well and was into regular classes fast. He really enjoyed the anatomy and physiology classes.

He was very lonely, so we told him to check out area churches, and then get involved in young adult groups, Sunday School, and evening activities. He made friends fast and had several he ran around with.

The only deficits I still saw were his eye problem (he wore glasses to see the board or far away things), and his numb-like tongue (he used tons of sauces on his food like A1, mustard, etc.). He never complained about broccoli or green beans, because he couldn't taste them. We found something positive here. Craig healed emotionally and spiritually during this time, and the Lord showed him he was self-sufficient: he cooked, cleaned, did laundry, and went to school full-time. He did very well on all his prerequisites. Craig was not suited to this career choice, so he left that setting and came home. He was confused as to why God sent him there, and I told Craig all I had seen God do. I reminded him that God had healed his eyes – even after that two-year mark. When you told us the story about your eyes, it made me laugh. It was so you Craig and your sense of humor. I didn't write it down, but I'll go from memory.

You were invited to a revival in one of the area churches by a friend who knew you had some vision problems since your accident. The problems were worse with more reading and studying at college. Your neuro-ophthalmologist had given you more exercises to do, but since it had been two years, we were probably going to have to deal with it. If your eyes did not improve, it would mean prism glasses.

Well, to make a long story short, you went to the revival, and God was there. He prompted you to go to the altar; at first, you were hesitant, but you eventually obliged. The pastor met you there, and after you told him what was going on, he prayed for healing. After the service, he told you there was a bright light around you, and you were shining in His radiance. When you went to study that weekend, your eyes were healed. You pitched your glasses into the shoe box at the top of your closet. Remember that I asked! I also reminded Him and thanked Him again.

You meet new peers and had a girlfriend. You and your Creator had worked out a whole lot of stuff you couldn't do around home. I reminded him his heart needed healing as well as his brain, and that's what God had done there.

Now what you asked: Your dad and I encouraged you to get a part-time job and enroll in our local community college, majoring in general studies. I asked you what your passion/love was, and I knew what you would say: criminal justice.

I told you to take a class or two and let God lead the way. You got an associates degree in criminal justice and were chosen the Outstanding Student in your program. You met your love there, got engaged, and married Sarah on July 20, 2002. Then you went to that big city seventy miles away.

At the writing of this book, Craig has worked in a couple of big city jails as a corrections officer. He wants to complete his criminal justice bachelor's degree. There is a little person now. Craig's focus is on providing a home (and all that means) so his wife can be a full-time mom. Will he get his dream? I am not sure – but I do know we must have dreams and goals, or we get stuck just living! Craig and Sarah are very active in their church, serving God and living for Jesus. He is a compassionate person who has a funny sense of humor. He tells others what God had done for him and God will do it for them.

Christmas 2006, Sarah, Miss Maddison, and Craig

God fulfilled the promise He gave us, while Craig was in his coma with only a two percent chance to live. "Those who wait upon the Lord shall renew their strength. They will soar on wings like eagles, they will run and not grow weary, they will walk and not faint" (Isaiah 40:31). I have found while watching Craig travel this path, the secret was "those who wait upon the Lord." I didn't want to wait – I wanted it to end today. He provided enough grace for each day. The wisdom came each day. The other secret was to submit to God's will, let Him go before, and prepare the way. He is the only one who is truly able to change things. God keeps His promises, but He does it His way. The trust issue took a while to restore, and I still have to practice it in other areas of my life.

I marvel at all God did. He sustained us every day with His grace, which I needed because I ran low on strength early in the journey. I have never been closer to the Lord than those three months at the big city training center, I am sorry to say. Jesus and I became best friends, and we talked all day!! Craig couldn't talk for weeks. I learned to listen better, as well as discern God's voice, His will, and His presence in profound ways. He led us into greater truth and understanding of His word. I had a front-row seat, observing a miracle.

To you other families who have taken a similar journey, trust in the Lord, and lean not on your own understandings. In all your ways, acknowledge Him, and He will direct your path. He won't make life easy (without pain), but He will be in it with you. (Proverb 3:5-6)

There was a big stretch of highway between here and that big city. One weekend, driving back to the hospital, Craig asked me about his girlfriend and why she didn't want to be his girlfriend anymore. I pointed to that median between the two roads and all the trees that blocked it from view. I told him it was still over there! This wreck had separated them, and each of them had a different road to get to their destiny. I said God was on both roads, but for now, we had to travel our own road together, yet alone, me as his mom and him as the "hurt" person. I told him I was sorry this all happened and I would go with him. We had to let the One-in-charge lead us to where He wanted us. Our road was less traveled than her road, or his other friends' roads, but God was still there, and we just had to let Him lead. He had allowed this in our lives, and He was the only one who could get us to His destination.

Craig had dedicated his life to the Lord early in life, and all I was able to do was be his cheerleader and teacher until he became an adult. I praise God I got up early every morning to meet him and his brother at the breakfast table. We did a devotion together before I sent them out into the world. I made some career choices that allowed me to do that! I am glad I did this because it was that foundation in Christ that brought Craig full circle. A few times, I almost lost my grip. God was waiting for me to let go; He had Craig and still does to this day: I can't make anything happen; only He can!!

If you don't know Jesus as Lord and Savior, let me tell you that He is the basis for peace in the storm. Jesus becomes the anchor, which must be secure before you reach the end of life or that storm. Jesus wants to be along in the journey, calling the shots in your life. I used to tell the kids in my children's church to know Jesus is as easy as your ABC's.

A – <u>Ask</u> Jesus to be in your life by <u>accepting</u> Him and doing it His way...<u>according</u> to the Bible.

B – <u>Believe</u> Him for who He says He is, and walk in it. <u>Believe</u> He is God's son-sent at Christmas as His Father's gift to mankind... so we would have forgiveness of sins. We had to have Christmas before we could experience Easter. Before we could experience Easter morning, Jesus had to die a horrible death to pay for <u>my</u> sin. Make it personal, because He is personal, and it is personal! That love allowed God to let His son be nailed to the cross, but He is alive today to help me and Craig…to heal our sons and daughters and all who need a touch.

C – To get all that, I must <u>Confess</u> – I need Him to forgive my sins. <u>Confess</u> I need Him because I truly do!! Look what He did for me – because I am His daughter, joint heir with His Son, and I have a secure place in Heaven. Jesus knows me, Linda, by name and I know…I am convinced He is able to bring about what He has for Craig…and for me.

Craig's Mom,
Linda

P.S. I am a very insignificant person in the scheme of things here on planet Earth…yet when I needed help for my son, Jesus was/is my intercessor before God the Father. I believed God for His promises, and I have wonderful Christian friends who prayed for us, and with us, believing God. Their encouragement through cards, letters, prayers, and acts of kindness to Paul and Michael while we were away those months and afterwards made the tragedy a journey of love and a miracle. God loves it when we run to Him for…everything. I will never know who each of you were, but I truly praise God and am thankful for all "your" prayers and the love you expressed in many ways. It is hard to put some things into words. I hope you gain hope through reading this.

That is my heart's desire.

Just a mom,
Linda

Yvonne's letter continues...

The first time we saw Craig was a whole different story, and the progress we saw was amazing. I will never understand all that went on and what you went through. I thank the Lord for seeing Craig back to health. Your testimonies are a blessing to those who hear them.

Love in Christ,
Yvonne

P.S. I want Craig to know that I take no credit for any of the miracles God did in his life. Looking back, I am grateful to have been just a little part of his life. Somehow, I have always felt a special bond with Craig since that night. I know he will be (and has been) a mighty spokesman for God. I will always pray for him – wherever God leads him.

Afterthoughts:

There were still many things I couldn't share; some things you don't even comprehend until later looking back. One for me was why didn't Craig have his seatbelt on, he had always worn it. He even thought he had put it on that night. Yet when I saw the pictures of the truck, I figured God had been there in that, too. Supposedly the truck rolled three times, yet Craig came out of it close to the road. If he hadn't, he would have been hurt much worse the way the cab was squashed down in that corner. Maybe he had it buckled and it came unbuckled. Maybe that was another way God protected him?

There were questions about this and that. One of the classmates found Craig's Bible in the field and it was open to a certain page. Was that significant – I don't remember much of these things! I know what God spoke and did for me, and I know some of the many things he did specifically for Craig, but we won't know it all till we get to Heaven, and probably not then. It won't matter then anyway.

To all you Christian parents out there, don't assume your children are exempt from a disaster. Make sure they have made a profession of faith in Jesus and attend a Bible-believing church that teaches the Word. Don't stop there! You are ultimately responsible for their Biblical instruction and accountability. Give them high standards; challenge them to be different for Jesus. Make sure they attend their Sunday services and have good Christian friends and peers to hang out with...at your house...so you know their friends and where they are at. Live your life with no regrets...our sons knew we loved them...we told them often and we knew their faith in their friend Jesus was real and authentic. If Craig would have died that night he would have been in Heaven. God had other plans and took us on a journey I never could have imagined...

To be honest, it has taken me a few years to work through some things...post traumatic shock syndrome I think they call it. Whenever I saw a helicopter land at the local hospital, I would find my heart racing and tears coming, because I knew a family was in an emergency life-threatening situation, and I knew the panic in their hearts. I knew their lives were changed forever. Ambulances rushing to an auto accident made me pray more for unknown people, but we would pray – you don't need names to send your petitions to Heaven. If writing this helps one person understand that someone else has been where they sit and it did turn out okay, that is my prayer.

Some days I felt guilty God answered so many of our prayers; we made it a practice to pray for all those around us. Sometimes people came to us to ask for prayer and we did pray right then for them.

We all have disappointments in life. We have to walk through it one-on-one with our Heavenly Father; only He can mend a broken heart, ease a broken dream, and give us a reason to press on. May all who read this book know that our God in Heaven is even on this road less traveled, and He is the only one who can travel any road with us...if we let Him. I pray that you do.

Craig's mom,
Linda

From Theo:

I hope, after reading this book you know miracles happen. You hear stories in the Bible about Jesus healing blind people, parting the Red Sea, or making the lame walk. The experience with Craig is something I will never forget. When you are only sixteen years old, knowing you might lose your best friend is very difficult. There even came a point when the doctors said he had a slim chance to live. I live about 1½ hours from the hospital, so I could not visit Craig as much as I would have liked, but we prayed everyday for whatever he needed prayer for, and Linda and Paul kept us informed throughout each day. God healed Craig to the point that you would never know he has ever had a horrific accident. I saw a miracle happen right before my eyes; I never doubted God could heal people, but when you see it up close in person, you really believe it. God is so real! Did God use Craig, so I could see a miracle? I also think God used Craig just to let us know life can be so short; sometimes we can take it all for granted. I would just like to say that I thank God everyday that He saved Craig's life and for those people who do not know God. Today, I pray that you will seek to know Him.

Craig, you are a great person of God, and I will always love you, man!

Theo

SPECIAL THANKS TO:

God Almighty*: for His Miracle for us, His Presence; His Holy Spirit.*

The Saints *– who prayed week after week.*

The doctors, nurses, and therapists *– who did their part and always "encouraged" Craig.*

Family and Friends *– who visited, sent cards, fixed meals, and took care of Paul and Michael at home.*

Bob and Ruth *– My pastor's parents who took me in for three months and were my home base and emotional support.*

Sue *– An L.D. teacher who went that extra mile for Craig, for us.*

Betty *– a long-time friend who typed this and retyped as we edited and edited.*

Thank you so much!

Linda Tegeler

Printed in the USA
CPSIA information can be obtained
at www.ICGtesting.com
LVHW041111050624
782358LV00014B/89